CAMPFIRE STORIES FOR KIDS: A SCARY GHOST, WITCH, AND GOBLIN TALES COLLECTION TO TELL IN THE DARK

Over 20 Scary and Funny Short Horror Stories for Children While Camping, Sleepovers

JOHNNY NELSON

Silk Publishing

INTRODUCTION

Thank you so much for picking this title to excite and thrill your child's imagination. These stories were written for children ages seven to thirteen, but adults may also enjoy them. They were written to make free time more exciting! There is something inside this book for everyone.

Spooky locations and fascinating characters make reading a blast. Each narrative was crafted to build a strong vocabulary while also keeping you on the edge of your seat. Halloween can be any time of the year, now. Dive into this book to find your new favorite story today.

This book is filled with tales of ghosts and ghouls. There are comedic selections and some that will make you consider the circumstances of your own life. Meet witches, evil teachers, and scary spirits. Can you solve the puzzles in time to save your friends? Would you turn your family pets into human beings if you could?

The next time you find yourself alone on a dark and stormy night, pick up this book. The next time you are in the mood to be a little scared, pick up this book. When you are looking for something different from everything else on the market, flip to a story, and get started. Find the thrill you have been craving. There are so many wonderful children's books on the market, thank you so much for giving this one a chance!

THE NEIGHBOR'S CAT

My neighbor, Claude, had never been a cat person. The older adult had said as much to me several times. He was always frustrated with our other neighbors for their love of pets.

Claude was a generally grumpy man. He spent all of his free time gardenings; he had an entire array of vegetables and herbs growing in neat rows, in his yard. He believed that the many cats in the neighborhood were out to destroy his plants.

Then, one day, a new stray appeared. The arrival of a new cat was nothing unusual, as we lived next to a highway. It was a prime unwanted pet-dumping area. We also had a neighbor named Amy, who liked to take the animals in after they were set out. *She* was a cat lady.

The stray was different, somehow. The animal immediately captured old Claude's heart. His name was Orphan (Claude named him). The cat seemed to have a certain amount of respect for the older adult's gardening. It would avoid the areas of the yard where he had planted.

Orphan was known as Ore, for short. The cat became famous around the neighborhood for how nice he was. Claude loved the animal so much that he would not let Amy take him. Instead, Claude fed Ore and let the stray live inside his house when Ore felt like coming in.

I enjoyed Ore's company too. Orphan was a solid black cat with bewitching green eyes and a ton of personality. I would sit outside on the front porch swing, finishing my homework every day. Orphan would rest beside me and just watch me work. It was almost as though he took an interest in whatever subject I happened to be studying.

One day, Claude passed away. I was sad. I cried as my mother hugged me, trying to calm me down. I had gotten so used to seeing and occasionally talking to Claude.

"Lindsey, have you heard?" My sister asked me one day, following his funeral.

"No, what?" I asked.

"As they were cleaning out Claude's house, they found some strange stuff. His daughter told me today. His family is visiting from New York to make sure that his belongings are packed up before they sell the house," she said.

"What? Wait. I thought Claude's daughter was missing?" I replied.

"No. His daughter's son (Claude's grandson) is missing. Everyone thinks he ran away," she said.

"What do you mean, strange stuff?"

"I mean they found magical spell books and other strange stuff. Ouija boards and candles were lying around the place. He used magic, and no one knew. Isn't that scary?" She asked.

"Yeah, I guess. Clause was still Claude, though, right? He was still the man I knew," I said.

"Sure, as much as you can know anyone."

There was a small fight over who was going to be allowed to keep the cat. Amy wanted the animal to add to her growing family of pets. I liked having him around. So, I talked my parents into asking if we could have Ore.

Orphan's new family was chosen in the silliest way. A person from each of the four homes who wanted to care for Ore stood apart at an equal distance. The poor meowing cat was put down in the center of that square. Whomever he walked over to would take him in. The only rule was that the winning family must allow the other neighbors to visit him.

That cat chose me, fair and square. I was going to have my pet, a downright beautiful pet, at that. I jumped up and down and clapped. I felt the whole competition was silly until I won.

Ore assimilated into our family well. He relaxed away most of his days in my room, curled up, by my side. I conversed with the cat as if he were a person. He would often seem to react to my words, making me feel insane.

"Ore, please don't lay on my laptop," I said. The cat politely stood up and moved himself to the floor.

Then things began to get a little creepy. At night, when I would sleep, the cat chose to rest on the floor beside my bed. In my dreams, I was in a strange house. From another room, I could hear a man yelling the same word over and over again. *Rosebush! Rosebush! Rosebush!*

I had never had the same dream more than once, in my entire life until that moment. Then the night-mare became more and more regular. Always with the little black cat sitting directly beside me. I would awaken to find Ore sitting on my bed, looking at me.

The predictable image began to send shivers

down my spine. The cat's actions became more and more bizarre. There was a book lying on my desk that the cat attacked endlessly. Ore spent his time clawing the cover of that dictionary-like he was trying to open it. The job was difficult for him because cats don't have thumbs.

The poor cat became extremely restless. Ore was always on edge. He was always running from one end of the house to the other. When someone would try to hold him, he'd act angry, and sometimes he even clawed. It was not like him at all. He had changed.

One day, I awoke to find the dictionary lying open on top of my desk. He was sitting directly behind the book, looking downward. I felt scared for a moment. It was as though my pet were trying to communicate with me.

The page was open to the 'R's section. There, I saw the word I'd heard in my dreams. There was a small tear in the page, beside the term.

"Rosebush," I said, glancing reluctantly at my cat.

He immediately began to intensity purr. *He is a strange animal. He enjoys hearing the word "Rosebush" spoken out loud.* How did he communicate that to me in my dream?

I heard the worst popping and cracking sounds. I looked at my cat, who was twisting and rolling around on top of my desk. The look in Ore's eyes told me that the animal was in pain. I could only watch in horror. I tried to comfort him, but my pets did not seem to work. There was nothing I could do. Ore was shaking.

Then his form began to change. I let out a scream as his fur began to fall off, and he grew larger and larger. My parents were not home, or else they might have heard me yelling. My heart was pounding, and I thought I might throw up.

It took about ten minutes before the change was complete. A young man lay upon my desk, shaking. I covered him with a blanket as I looked on, shocked and confused.

"C...C...Claude," was all he could manage to say. I finally began to understand. Claude, who seemed to know all about magic and spells. The older adult whose grandson disappeared under mysterious conditions. The man had even named his cat "Orphan."

"He hated me. I made him angry. He loved his daughter enough not to hurt me, but he didn't want me around to bother him. He was upset because he was stuck babysitting me all the time. He could not stand it.

"One day, when I was playing, I fell into his Rosebush, breaking several branches with flowers. I had never seen him that angry. I must have blacked out. I woke up trapped in a new body, the body of a cat," Ore said. He was finally able to pull himself together. "I wish I could explain this madness. Trying to get someone to say a word without being able to speak was almost impossible. I thought that I might lose my mind. I thought maybe I had already."

"You appeared to me in my dreams," I said, amazed.

"I don't know how but I am glad that it happened," Ore said. The young man spent the next few hours recovering from the events. He showered and ate a human meal for the first time in a year. Then he called his mother and told her to come and get him. I could hear her crying over the phone.

When my mother came home, and I told her that Claude's grandson had somehow found his way over to our house. He introduced himself as Steven, telling her that he had run away but was now returning home. His mother was already on the way to pick him up. Our excuses did not make much sense, but mom only questioned us for a moment before moving on.

She poured food into Orphan's bowl and began to call him. I was going to have to come up with another excuse for the missing cat. Then she turned to Steven, and I began to make small talk.

"I saw the most beautiful rosebush today, on the way home from work..." I glanced at Steven, who seemed as though he might throw up. Even if I had never said the words, myself, he still would have been set free. It was fate.

❧ 2 ❧

SUSURROUS

Freddie's grandparents lived on isolated land located deep within a forest. Throughout Freddie's childhood, he had been afraid to visit them, even though their family was very tight-knit. Their small farmhouse did not seem to offer enough protection from the frightening woods that surrounded the home.

The young man had never experienced anything that could be considered ghostly, but he was weirdly afraid of the entire area around his grandparent's home. Forests, in general, upset him. He would spend nights at their house, occasionally. Freddie would attempt to fall asleep on their pull-out couch as he listened to the sounds coming from outside. He imaged they were coming from a forest monster.

His young mind would race as he laid there in the darkness. Freddie would dream up frightening monsters with fangs like knives and red eyes that glowed brightly into the dark. He shook beneath his blankets, pulling the fabric up over his face.

Soon, the air beneath his blankets would become too hot to breathe comfortably. His heart would race as he had to think about lowering the sheets and facing the unknown monsters in the darkness. Neither choice was excellent.

Freddie was sure that the moment he pulled his head from beneath, he'd find himself face to face with a nightmare. The young man dreaded the dark and the imaginary unblinking eyes that must have been watching him, waiting for their chance to strike.

These nights were the product of childhood imagination. Imaginations can work wonders with pure fear. The outline of the stack of clothes upon a chair, in the darkness, becomes a monster standing silently and waiting. The creaking of wood in the stillness of night changes into a dangerous stranger hanging around just outside the door.

Freddie was ashamed that he had ever feared his imagination. He had always been the friend that could not ride the roller coaster and was afraid to break the rules. Childhood should be fun. You are supposed to have fun and not worry, Freddie believed. That was not the way his mind worked, and it had never been. He was cautious and careful.

One summer, the young man decided that he was no longer going to be ashamed of himself. He decided that he was going to face all of his fears. Freddie would leave no stone unturned. He was no longer a child, after all.

Freddie confronted his most common worries, first. He placed himself in situations during which he would be forced to be brave. Riding rollercoasters, climbing rock walls, ice skating, and swimming in the ocean, his summer was full of activities that had always caused him to freeze.

It was during one of those hot summer days that Freddie and his mother set off to visit his grandparents. Freddie had so much he wanted to tell his grandfather. Freddie felt as though he were finally becoming the man that he had been meant to be, someone of whom his family could be proud of.

The sight of the forest no longer scared him. There was no knot in his stomach, waiting to become untangled. The trees merely looked like bark and foliage; they no longer kept dangerous secrets. As his mother's car swerved to miss potholes in the long dirt road, he sighed. It was as though he was aware of nature's calm and overwhelming beauty, in those woods, for the first time.

That night, the family sat around the small dining table. In between bites of a delicious casserole, he told his grandfather stories about his adventures. Freddie and his friends had recently set out upon a weekend-long camping trip. The boys had told scary stories by the light of a crackling fire in the night. He recounted the smell of the smoke as it filled his nose and stung his eyes.

There was a light in his grandfather's eyes while he explained his love of camping. Many of the days of his childhood occurred in the mountains. His grandfather had played in the many creeks and watched the animals as they went about their day.

"Have you ever camped here? You have so much land. It's perfect for camping!" Freddie asked.

"No, actually," his grandfather's smile was briefly replaced by a look of worry and amusement. "You are going to think I am crazy, but I am afraid of this forest at night. There is a local ledged that made me think twice about wandering around out there," he said. Freddie felt the familiar feeling of fear rising in his stomach. He almost didn't want to ask.

"Why? What is the legend?" Freddie's mother asked.

"It's silly," his grandmother said.

"They say that once a year, the forest comes to life in the night. Words were heard coming from the tree line, inviting those on the outside to come into the woods," his grandfather replied.

"What? What is inside?" Freddie asked with a gulp.

"No one knows. No one has ever accepted the invitation."

"When does all this happen?" Asked Freddie.

"The night before Halloween."

Freddie left that night feeling scared again. He'd thought he was done with fear. Freddie had been right about the forest for his entire childhood. He hated being correct about all of those nights, with the blankets pulled up above his head. Even more than that, he hated that he knew he had to face the fear.

He told his mother on the drive home. Freddie explained to her that he was going to have to see for himself. She immediately said no, to keep him from venturing out into harm's way. He asked over and over again, as the following months passed. Eventually, she gave in. When she finally agreed to let him chase his last great fear, she gave him conditions. She was to join him. Planning for his mother's presence put his mind at ease a little. He was also not going to be allowed to leave the tent without her.

She did not believe in ghosts or monsters. Her even presence always comforted Freddie, even during full-blown panic attacks. Freddie knew that she would be able to instantly explain away anything unusual that the pair might experience that night.

In the months that followed, he tried to learn about the local legend, more. There was little information to be found online. Freddie also wanted to prepare himself for their stay. He and his friends camped more often; slowly, he became more comfortable in the forest at night.

When the day arrived, Freddie and his mother ate dinner with her parents; there were exciting conversations and predictions. His grandfather seemed worried, insisting that they come inside the moment they felt unsafe. The pair placed their tent at the edge of the clearing, right in front of the tree line.

The seasons had changed since he had last visited. It was autumn, and the land around their tent was lovely. Freddie felt a little better, being surrounded by such beautiful views.

The woods were beautiful. The yellow and orange leaves had mostly fallen to the forest floor. A sweet and earthy smell rose from the ground. The scent of fall kicked up with every step they took. The breeze carried with it a chill. The cold only became more intense as the day faded into darkness.

The change into night brought with it a general spookiness that raised the hairs on Freddie's arms. He shook as his mother sat reading a book on the other end of the tent. As the hours passed, he became more at ease. He was even able to fall asleep at around midnight when nothing had happened, something he would never have been able to do, only a year before.

Freddie was awoken from his dreams, by a soft sound. The wind surrounded the tent, disturbing the fabric walls. The noise faded into the background at first, but then he heard it.

A low musical whisper called out through the night. It called him to come forth into the trees. It drew a name that he had never heard before, but he felt the words pulling him. Icy terror gripped his mind, but his body was moving on its own, following the orders. Freddie felt a hot tear fall from his cheek as he walked out of the tent. He wanted to cry. He had never been so frightened in his life.

Through the trees, he walked. The leaves crunched beneath his shoes. The young man's fear turned to intense sadness as he continued along the path that he was following. He could not explain the feeling. It was not rooted in his reality, but *something else's*.

Then he saw her. A sad little girl stood glowing in a clearing before him. She held something, maybe a dog's collar. Tears streamed from her eyes too until she saw Freddie. A small smile made it's way across her lips as her cheeks were still shining from the ghostly tears.

Freddie *felt* her thoughts. She was so happy and pleased to see him. Her clothing was strange, old, and worn out. It seemed as though she had been roaming around the forest for eternity.

He knew that he was not in danger. There was no anger directed toward him. The little ghost girl must have been calling for her lost dog. Freddie walked toward the sad child and then sat down beside her. He was face-to-face with the unknown ghost that he had been so afraid of for all those years. The poor child was nothing except for innocence and sadness.

Freddie stayed with the girl until the early hours of dawn. The pair did not speak, but he knew that she was glad for the company. It had been so long. She was not of this world, but the one beyond. The young man felt connected to the ghost's very fragile and very human emotional state.

Every year, Freddie returned to that spot. He camped in the forest behind his grandparent's house on the night before Halloween. Freddie waited for his eternally tiny friend to appear with tears rolling across her glowing cheeks. Every year, he stopped her tears by being present. His secret weapon helped in this mission too.

The young man convinced his mother to let him adopt a puppy, which he named Minster. Freddie got the idea for the moniker from the youthful spirit in the forest. It was the name she had called out through the darkness. Minster brightened the face of that little girl for one night of every following year.

3

WISTFUL

The old hotel laid abandoned for over eighty years. The business had operated since the 1950s. Its empty rooms rested still and silent for all to see, a ghost to the passing years. The building was beautiful in its prime, a jewel in the crown of downtown Aimsbury.

Below the crumbling hotel, an antique shop operated on the ground level of the building. A ladder in the back of the store could be pulled from the ceiling to allow access to the stories above. There were very few willing to make the trip up to the old Jewel Hotel.

The floorboards were broken and falling apart. Walking across the old hotel floors was dangerous. There was a chance that you might just fall through the old wood.

There was minimal trace of the majesty that once lived within that structure. There was no more front desk, and the rooms had all been torn apart. There was even an old lounge where guests could come to watch performers sing. You would have never been able to guess its previous purpose.

Light flowed in through windows that were covered with falling newspaper. The dust floated through the air like a thick fog. It rose and fell as it was disturbed. You could often hear the wind outside, being cut by the corners of the tall building.

The creepiest part of the whole experience was the birds. Crows had somehow found their way into the old hotel. Some of them were also able to find their way back out. Their presence added a dark décor.

Mason got a job in the antique shop below because he had a love for items with a history. There had always been magic in aged objects, according to the young man. He liked to run his hands over the store's new inventory and imagine the story of all the people who owned it before he'd touched it. Mason's imagination was lively.

His active imagination was the reason he doubted himself the first time he heard the music. Mason was closing the store when he heard sounds coming from the levels up above him. He had never been to the abandoned hotel before and was frightened by the idea that something was up there making a sound, so he hurried home rather than checking it out. The young man thought that he might perhaps be going crazy.

Another night, the young man heard a low melody floating down from the rafters. Mason was more curious that day. Pieces of an incomplete song rang out through the night. He knew that he was going to explore because adventure-seeking was in his nature.

Mason found the ladder without searching for very long. He pulled it down and slowly climbed up into the abandoned building. There was no light, so he was forced to use the flashlight on his dying phone.

Now and then, he was struck by a sudden noise, frozen in place. Mason would turn to see a bird flapping or the tail-end of a sprinting mouse. The young man then laughed at himself for being so jumpy.

From the corner of his eye, he saw something moving across an open doorway. Mason's blood ran cold. The air around him also became chilly. He could barely move. He was half sure that he was going insane and half convinced that he was about to be eaten by a monster.

Then the music began to play again. The soft notes of a piano rang out through the blackness. The melody was slow, at first. It grew to be quicker and more intense as time went on.

Mason gathered up his nerve and began to look around. Suddenly, the light from his phone turned off, and he stumbled onto the ground. There were sounds all around him, but the music stopped for a moment. He was terrified. How was he going to get back down? Was he going to be hurt? Could he be fired for hanging out up here? His head throbbed with pain.

The young man shut his eyes as he felt himself beginning to panic. Then he heard the lovely voice of a woman. No piano played behind her song. It was just her low and angelic voice. She hummed for a moment before breaking out into song.

It was a troubled song, one of war and loss. Mason could feel the sadness of her tone. The words she sang reached deep inside and touched the young man's soul. He opened his eyes to see her. The world around him was still damaged and old, except for her. She existed in brilliant glowing color. Her universe was slowly expanding out from her, turning the building new again, and rewinding time.

Mason watched as she swayed back and forth. She was standing on a small stage in front of a crowd. The young woman was wearing a shining green gown with long gloves. People watched her from tables unevenly spaced throughout the other end of the dimly lit room. Some of the people smiled and clapped. Others minded their drinks and their cigars, filling the room with smoke. The leftover hotel guests chatted amongst one another, barely lifting their heads.

The woman on the microphone did not seem to mind. She was in her world, singing to herself. He could tell that her mind was somewhere else. Then, from the back of the room, a man appeared. He wore a soldier's uniform. She stopped in the middle of her song to run and throw herself into his arms.

He took off his hat as he held her, and the pair spun around. The man then placed his arm around her and walked her back to the stage. She was crying tears of joy. She was beautiful, with big brown eyes and scarlet hair fashioned into tiny waves against her head. The man was also handsome in his army green uniform. He had a kind face, one that had probably seen unfair horror. His heart seemed to belong entirely and totally to the woman. He called her Maggie Greensleeves.

The darkness slowly overtook Mason's vision again. When the figures reemerged, it was not such a pleasant scene. He saw the same room, except this time, it was mostly empty. Staff in grey dresses shuffled about, getting things ready for the evening. The mood was different.

Maggie sat alone at a table in a pale rose-colored dress. Her glowing skin highlighted her within the black room. Fate had intervened, Mason felt as though he was destined to see her. The young man appeared again in his army uniform; her lover held a bouquet of orange roses. Maggie smiled weakly. The couple was saying their goodbyes.

Mason felt a sorrow deep within his stomach that he could not stand. He could sense their longing and sadness. When the handsome man in the uniform had to leave, Maggie buried her face within the roses. Her tears rolled into the flowers. They would see each other again; Mason felt that in his soul. But that moment had been filled with such intensity that it had left its mark upon the old hotel. His vision faded again.

Mason awoke lying on the floor in the antique shop. His boss explained to him that he fell and hurt his head the night before. They had to go and get him from the old hotel above. The thing she asked next, shocked him. She wondered if he had heard the beautiful voice singing. Was that why he had gone upstairs? He had thought that it was all some weird dream until she brought up the music.

Mason looked into Maggie Greensleeves. The moniker turned out to be a stage name given to a local performer named Margret Hollifield. The young man set out on his mission.

He arrived at the cemetery with a bouquet of orange roses in his hands. Mason had no trouble finding her gravestone. He felt led to it. She rested beside a man named Peter Hollifield, her love.

Mason laid the flowers upon her grave, gently. He thought of her lovely voice and her charming spirit. She had such an intense presence that she changed all the spaces where she'd existed. She altered that old hotel, making it into something beautiful. The entire building was now a love letter to her heart.

✣ 4 ✣

BAD MOON

Grandma Maybelle had always been a little kooky. She was born in the 1940s, but she dressed as though she'd hopped right out of the Victorian era. I remember being in love with her pretty dresses when I was young before I understood the insanity behind her wardrobe choices. Steamy Georgia summers in layers of thick old cloth; I had no idea how she lived like that.

She had my mother, Helen, late in her life and had given her up right after her birth. None of us knew the reason, but it was probably for the best. Mom had a wonderful childhood with some sane folks who lived in the correct century.

Maybelle had gotten in touch with my mother when she was already an adult. Mom tried to bond with her, but the pair did not have too much in common. We would spend hours on the road to visit her at her large musty house, only to be sent back home at the end of the day. We never stayed for more than six hours.

My grandmother's home was a worn-down Victorian-style mini-mansion. It was probably considered fancy in its prime. I can remember the smell of damp wood and mildew as I nervously wandered from room to room, walking around the piles of junk and old newspapers. I could not help but imagine the ghosts who must have traveled around the winding hallways alongside me.

There was a darkness that settled in amongst the stacks of old magazines. The windows were covered with cardboard and tape. Daylight and night looked similar inside the strange house. Not knowing the actual time made me feel uneasy, even as a child.

When mom received the news that Maybelle had passed away, she cried briefly. I could tell that she felt guilty about not being more moved by the event. I imagine she felt that way because I sure did.

Our family also received news that her large ghost hotel of a house was left to us. Both my mother and I were nervous about being stuck with the responsibility and the mountains of trash. My stepfather, Jim, was overjoyed. He loved a project and was sure that we could return the property to its former beauty. He had always felt a strange connection to Maybelle; the pair got along so well.

It was his misguided excitement that led to our

family's long summer stay in Castle Crap-ula. The entire town was weird. You could feel it the moment you passed the "Welcome to Moon" sign. I was over-come with the sensation of strange electricity as it ran across the surface of my skin, causing the hairs on my arms to stand straight up.

"Jenny, you are overdramatic!" Jim said, turning around from the front seat of the car. "The people here are so nice. We are going to renovate, relax and maybe even make some new friends. I might even learn how to cook; you never know!" I held my tongue.

The house was located in the middle of a historic downtown area, in a town simply called Moon. It wasn't the familiar bustling city, which was going to be an adjustment, but the area wasn't wholly country either. I was sure that I could find something to fill my time here. Maybe a cute coffee shop or a shady trail through the local park could become my new haunts.

As we pulled into the driveway, our car tires crackled atop the hot pavement. Neighbors to our side looked up from their gardening. They made a beeline for our car, excited to introduce themselves. The pair was healthy-looking enough. If I were to guess at their jobs, I would have said lawyer or accountant.

They lived in a similarly old home, except theirs was more colonial styled and had been well maintained. I tuned their conversation out as I looked around. It had been two years since we'd visited. I spoke to Maybelle on the phone much more often than in person. She was a sweet lady. I should have made more of an effort.

My parents finished their short discussion with the neighbors, and we all made our way up the stone stairs to the front door. My mother fumbled with the keys as my stepfather snickered. He seemed amused.

"They told us never to leave the house after the sun went down. Something about crime in the area being out of control. They freaked your mom out," said Jim when we were all finally inside. Small clouds of dust rose around us, as our movement disturbed the scary stillness.

"They just seemed...off? I don't know. It was not like they were suggesting that we not go out late. They *told* us that we couldn't. They said that the Moon shuts down, and the streets become dangerous. The wife also said that we should not even draw the curtains or turn on a porch light; violent criminals might target us," said mom.

"I told you that this place was weird. The whole town of Moon is strange," I said.

"The lady said we were not even supposed to look outside. I believe she might be a little paranoid. Besides, I am here to protect you ladies from the criminal element!" Jim said. I could not help but smile because he was so goofy.

Despite the lighthearted nature of my parent's tone that day, we did not leave the house after dark. A strange howling came from outside. It almost sounded like the wind, at first. But it was not. There was something primitive and frightening about the noise. It was as though the sound was pretending to be from nature but was not natural.

The house, which had, at first, seemed frightening, suddenly became a safe place. It vibrated and creaked, as though we were in the middle of an intense storm. We sat in the living room, listening to the sounds coming from the darkness outside. No one said it, but I could tell that we were each engaged in mental gymnastics. We were trying to make the noises make sense. The howling was surely just the wind, right?

Jim began to walk toward one of the cardboard covered windows. I was filled with a growing sense of dread as he inched closer and closer to the covering. My mom was the first to yell, "STOP!" but if she hadn't, I would have. He paused and made a joke about first night jitters, claiming we would all feel silly in the morning.

I did feel silly suppose silly meant like an unrested ball of nerves. I was staying in a guest bedroom that I had never been allowed to sleep in before. I covered my ears beneath the thick quilts and waited out the night. The howling faded away at around six a.m.

I looked through the house for clues, carefully

making my way through the dusty corridors looking for anything that wasn't an old newspaper or magazine. The massive stacks of books hindered my search. These books took up much of the space in the cluttered rooms; the whole job took more energy than I had available. I was exhausted.

I knew then that clearing all of that mess out, was going to be a nightmare. I riffled through piles of papers and other reading materials. It was as though Maybelle had been obsessed with reading information. Like she was creating an external library.

I explained to my mother that I was looking for journals or other personal effects of Maybelle. She joined me in my job. We worked through her bedroom.

At the top of the closet, we found a stack of journals hidden in a large cardboard box. Maybelle had not added to the collection for some time, and they were quite old. Could there have been more somewhere?

Mother let me take the stack so that I could study them in my free time. We spent the rest of the day coming up with a plan for clearing the house. We were going to have to go through the massive amount of clutter, bit by bit.

That night, the howling returned. I heard my mom yelling at my stepdad to keep away from the windows. She loudly explained that they would ask the neighbors, tomorrow, to explain further about the supposed crime. Until then, he needed to stop. His curiosity was going to get him into trouble.

I was in the middle of reading through the journals. They were from around the time Maybelle was pregnant with my mother. She called herself Ellen, in those notebooks, Ellen was such a strange nickname. She made some nonsensical choices for someone who was otherwise intelligent and articulate. Maybelle seemed like a completely different person in her writing. She and her husband were looking forward to my mother's birth.

Maybelle wrote that they had just purchased a large old Victorian house with a lot of "personality." The town was quiet, but the people were a little strange. As they were moving in, they were told to keep away from the dark, but the reasons were different.

Upon their first night in the house, they heard the howling. Distant screaming permeated through the walls of the house. My grandmother was much more intelligent than I had been, in the pursuit of information. She bribed someone in town to reveal the source of the dreadful noise to her. Maybelle had to search all day for a person who was willing to tell her the truth. The man extorted her into paying hundreds of dollars for an explanation.

August 1st, 1979

It turns out that the entire town of Moon is insane, Diary. The man I paid told me that the city was cursed. The night belonged to spirits of the past. They roam the streets, waiting for a fresh host. Whenever someone makes the mistake of looking at them, the phantoms receive an invitation to take over the body. Their howls, he said, are calls trying to tempt the locals into looking outside. Am I to assume that everyone in town is crazy enough to believe this? I should have done more research before I bought this house.

August 9th, 1979

Dan, my husband, has been taken. He believes he is a pilot from 1945. Please tell me that this is a sick joke. He wants me to refer to him as Gerald. I am to give birth next month. What on earth am I to do?

September 21st, 1979

Her name is Helen.

She was adopted by Sarah and Daniel Graham of TN. (Their address and personal information listed here). *Please make sure she is given the money from this house when I perish. Never allow her to come here.*

That was the last entry. I was thoroughly confused by the words I had just read. I did not understand. I was so tired that I could not swallow that information. I began to fight sleep, as my eyelids became heavy. It was as though I was being relieved of my duty to figure the puzzle out.

The following morning, I heard laughter coming from the kitchen. I held the journal clutched tightly to my chest. I had to show my parents. I had to warn them. Maybe they could tell me that Maybelle (or

Ellen) was crazy. Perhaps they could explain this to me.

The sound of my mother's laugh was musical. It filled the dusty halls of the house, as did the smell of her breakfast. The scent was beautiful. I hadn't realized I was starving until that moment. I entered the room to see my mother's smiling face. I hugged her as she sat in a chair, pulled against the kitchen bar.

"Wait... you aren't cooking?" I asked her. My mother smiled at me and placed a hand on my shoulder. Jim stood before the stovetop, wearing an apron. My heart dropped. The world around me began to spin.

"I am the chef this morning, kiddo! Pancakes for everyone!" Jim said.

"It's weird, right? He said he suddenly remembered a blueberry pancake recipe, so he is treating us! He has even made sausage and eggs. What an improvement," Mom joked.

My body was frozen with fright. My pulse quickened as my heart pounded against my ribcage. There was no point in showing them the journal. I could not hear anything else she said to me through the dizziness. Jim had always been so helpless with food. He could not even cook TV dinners.

5

GEMINI HOUSE

Bailey had heard rumors about the old country club, long before she ever worked there. The place was so exciting. There had been so much history, drama, and life to play out beneath the roof of the Ivy Country Club. The wealthiest people in her town had always been full of strange secrets.

The young woman's application to the summer program had been accepted. She would be responsible for cleaning up after the guests. She was going to have a chance to get a look at the inner workings of a country club.

Not to mention, Ivy Country Club had a storied past. There were rumors that the place was filled with ghosts or that it had a personality of its own. It seemed to really dislike some patrons and enjoy others. The building showed favoritism.

That was the most exciting thing that Bailey had heard. People in town called the club "Gemini House" because of the many personalities that it seemed to exhibit. There were so many tales of the building locking patrons out or causing fixtures to fall from the ceilings on unwitting guests below. Ironically, the place rumored to hate gossip.

Guests have reported feeling the temperature in the room switch from hot to cold, instantly. They would go from burning up, to watching their breath. The stories creeped Josh, Bailey's friend, out. The young woman, however, was fearless. She was brave and fascinated, which can be a dangerous combination.

Bailey wanted to see something scary. She wanted to see a ghost. The paranormal excited her, and the young woman was ready to take on the task of working in the Gemini House. She had even spoken to management and gotten Josh hired for the summer months too.

One day, a birthday party was held within the building. Lots of wealthy guests stayed until late at night. Bailey and Josh were on the cleanup crew for the event. Josh was nervous while Bailey was excited. Management told them to try not to get stuck in the club after nine p.m., but she didn't know if they were joking. When the clock struck ten p.m., she knew she was going find out.

Bailey and Josh worked with the other staffers.

They all had an obscenely early shift in the morning. One young lady suggested that they all just find a room out of the way. They could sleep at the club for the night. Josh was deadest against this idea, but he didn't want to look weak, so he didn't say anything. Most of the other staffers felt the same way. They also said nothing.

That night, they all chatted and joked until everyone fell asleep, except for Bailey. She awoke Josh at three a.m. to go walking around. When he refused, she said she would go alone. He sighed and pulled himself from his warm, safe sleeping bag.

The friends began to explore the dark hallways. Each one was scarier than the last, Josh thought. Bailey was acting utterly unaffected until the music rang out through the halls. A lady's voice shook the ground. The sound of glass breaking shot through the darkness.

Bailey froze, and so did Josh. He readied himself to run back to the room where he was safe. Bailey was frightened, but more than that, she was curious. She continued down the long hall toward the song. Josh followed her.

She reached the auditorium. So many sounds came behind those double doors. Josh tried to reach out and stop his friend, but she was too fast. She pulled the handle and opened the door.

Josh thought that he might pass out. His whole

body was shaking. The young man was not ready for whatever lay on the other side of those doors.

The sight inside was beautiful. It was not like anything either of the friends had ever laid eyes on before. The entire room was alight with glowing ghosts, as they danced gracefully across the floor. The gowns for the ladies were long and swaying. The light shined through the transparent pastel dresses.

The men looked dapper in their tailored suits. The gentlemen led their partners in the dance. On the stage, there was a piano player and a stunning opera singer. She was belting out notes in the most elegant way.

Bailey and Josh gasped. A ghostly figure in a long blue dress motioned for the pair to join. The friends spent that night dancing with ghosts. It turned out that there had been an incident in the club many years ago. Now beautiful spirits occupied so much of the building. The ghosts all looked like enchanted light paintings.

They were not angry. The ghosts were not picking people to mock. Bailey could feel their energy, and it was playful. They picked on the humans in good fun. At night, they danced their ghostly cares away. That night, Bailey and Josh danced right along with them.

❧ 6 ❧

UNLUCKY CHARM

Mr. Agate tapped his pen against his desk. The new teacher was an oddball, that was for sure. The man's smile was both disarming and worrying. He taught world history but did so excitingly and engagingly.

Still, there was something off about the man. The mischievous shine in his eyes made him seem eternally youthful. The way he spoke was careful, as though he practiced his words in his mind before they ever had the chance to escape from his mouth. The excited tone of his voice seemed to contrast the care he seemed to take when choosing his words.

Mr. Agate was always sharply dressed, wearing only dark colors. He was young for a teacher at my school. Girls in my class swooned as he walked by, which I found to be terminally annoying. Their attention seemed to be the fault of his charm.

I enjoyed his class more than any other. I learned the subject with ease because he turned each lesson into a conversation. I was also at odds with myself because something about the man just wasn't right.

"You're just jealous, Stan," said Rose, one of my closest friends. She must have noticed the look that I was giving the man.

"I didn't even say anything," I whispered back to her.

"You are looking at the teacher like you hate him," she said.

"I don't hate him. I just don't trust him," I said. He had only been working at my school for a few months. Mr. Agate had blown into town and immediately gotten a job as a teacher. I had a right to worry about strangers.

"I agree with Stan. Something is weird about him. I wouldn't be surprised if he led a life of crime before coming here," Carlos, our other stooge, chimed in. There was no way that Mr. Agate heard us, but he turned and flashed us a warning glance. "He has lizard ears," Carlos added.

"I am pretty sure lizards don't have ears," I said.

"Lizards absolutely have ears. What did you think those holes in the side of their heads were?" Rose asked.

"I don't know. I don't study reptiles," I said.

"Guys, what if the teacher is a reptile?" Carlos asked. The volume of his voice did not reach more than a hushed whisper. Mr. Agate struggled to hold back laughter. There is no way he could have heard us.

"Reptilian humans don't exist. Who do you get your information from?" Rose asked, at the end of class when she finally felt safe to speak again. Before Carlos could answer, Mr. Agate called on a student named Ralph to meet with him after class.

The following day in class, I listened passively to the lesson. Mr. Agate was speaking about the Roman Empire with his usual excitement. My gaze was not on the teacher that day, but in the direction of Ralph.

Ralph looked rough. The young man had scarcely spoken a word since the beginning of class, which was unusual. His friends were attempting to talk to him, but he just stared straight ahead at nothing. His eyes were sunken in, as though he had not slept in days.

Ralph's skin was weirdly pale, and he looked all around sickly. My mind kept returning to the previous day. He had stayed after class with Mr. Agate. What if the teacher did something to turn him into a quasi-zombie? What if he took all his energy?

"What do you think is wrong with Ralph?" Asked Rose, following my eyes again. I shrugged, not wanting to tell her about my new conspiracy theory.

"What if Mr. Agate zonked him?" Asked Carlos. Rose rolled her eyes.

That day, following the lesson, he called on Rose

to meet him after class. He said that he wanted to discuss a paper that she had turned in earlier that week. I tried to interject, telling the teacher that Rose couldn't stay because she had an emergency and she was busy. She laughed off my excuse, telling Mr. Agate that I was making a joke. My friend waved me away.

I had tried so hard to stop her from going, but I could not just physically hold her back. She met with Mr. Agate. Worried, Carlos and I left. All we could do was hope for the best and monitor the situation.

Neither Carlos nor I were able to reach her after class. It wasn't until the next day that we were able to see Rose again. She looked like a walking Zombie, in the same way, Ralph still did. She was pale and sickly with sunken eyes. She did not respond to any of my questions. Rose was only able to listen to the lesson and write down her exercises.

Carlos and I were immediately suspicious. During this circumstance was the one time I felt lucky for having a conspiracy theorist friend. I just knew that Mr. Agate was responsible. I knew what I had to do.

When school ended that day, I did not take the bus home. I told my mother that I had a project I had to finish, and it was going to take me at least a few hours. She agreed to give both Carlos and I a ride home.

There were plenty of afterschool programs and other activities that required the student's presence in the halls. We would not stand out, so long as we looked like we were on our way to something. I told Carlos to walk around looking like he had somewhere important to be. He must have misunderstood because he instead thrust his shoulders back and took extra wide steps.

We waited until the areas around us were mostly clear before sneaking down the corridor where the history classrooms sat. That particular hallway was utterly dead. There was no one else around.

I quickly made my way over to Mr. Agate's room, with Carlos in tow. There was a vertical rectangular window built into the door of every classroom. It was no surprise that Mr. Agate covered his with construction paper. I stooped down with my eye squinted and peered through the keyhole in the doorknob.

Through the tiny hole in the doorknob, I could make out a small area of activity inside the classroom. A male student sat in a chair pulled up to the desk of Mr. Agate. The pair appeared to be engaged in conversation. The teacher was smiling and also seemed to be pointing out a passage in a textbook.

The student took the book from Mr. Agate and began to read the section, as he was told. As the young man continued, Mr. Agate pulled a necklace from behind his button-up shirt. From the end of the chain hung an amulet.

Mr. Agate used the student's distracted state to stand up and walk behind the young man with the charm hidden inside his closed palm. With the speed of a viper, he slapped the amulet against the boy's forehead. His opposite hand supported the back of his victim's head, ensuring that he escape the attack. The student started shaking. His body trashed as the necklace vacuumed up all of his energy. Or lifeforce?

I gasped, and Carlos demanded to know what I was seeing. I shushed him, but it was too late. Mr. Agate looked toward the closed door. He turned his attention from the student to us. The sinister teacher began to stroll toward the door, as he placed his necklace back in its place, around his neck.

"Follow my lead," I whispered to Carlos.

"What?" He asked.

I stood up quickly as the door opened; my heart was racing. That man had some sort of super-secret life-sucking weapon. I prepared myself for the end of my weird short life. I took a deep breath to steady my pulse, to no avail.

"Can I help you guys?" Mr. Agate asked, smiling mischievously at my friend and I. The half-zombie student was still sitting in the seat behind him, and Mr. Agate was acting as though everything was completely normal.

"Yes sir, we had a question about the homework," I said. Carlos stared at me with horror in his expression.

"Sure, why don't you guys come inside?" He asked.

I followed him into the classroom. The way

Carlos was tugging on my shirt sleeve told me that there was no homework. I waited until he closed the door behind us before making my move. I only had one idea to execute.

I reared back as Mr. Agate looked at me with confusion. I punched my teacher in the face. Carlos shrieked as the man doubled over but did not fall.

Carlos joined me in the assault, probably assuming he had no other option. He was always a good friend. I had never been in a physical fight before, but he had. Mr. Agate finally fell to the ground, stunned. I grabbed the necklace with the gemstone amulet and ripped it from around his throat. It looked so mundane.

Mr. Agate realized what was happening. I could feel the sudden shock of rage that rose through him. He began to pick himself up from the ground, and I turned to my friend and yelled.

"RUN!" And we did; Mr. Agate was right behind us, around every twist and turn. The alien teacher was relentless; I had only one idea left. We dashed through the hallways, passing worried onlookers. The teacher called for us to halt.

We led the teacher all the way downstairs. I ran into a classroom, and Mr. Agate followed me. I clutched the amulet as I bounded over desk after desk. I motioned for Carlos to go back toward the door. I wasn't sure if he understood, as I could usually bank on him, not understanding.

I threw the necklace into the hallway from the other side of the room. The lock on this particular door had been installed incorrectly. One could only open it from the outside. I knew because I had been placed in the class last semester. I hoped, more than anything, that the school had not repaired the door.

"Take it to the shop! Destroy it!" I screamed. I could tell by the look on Carlos's face that he was worried about leaving me with the homicidal teacher. "GO!"

Carlos slammed the door, locking us in the classroom. He ran down the hall. Mr. Agate dashed over to the threshold and began trying to leave. The doorknob would not budge. He realized that he was stuck inside with me. He slowly turned around.

"Do you have any idea what you have done?! Or what I'll do to you for it? My source of energy! You have stolen it," he sneered. No silly smile this time.

"You steal it! You turned my friend into a zombie!"

"I am going to end you and your little friends," he said. His words were venomous.

Mr. Agate took his time walking over to me. My pulse raced. He picked up a portable pencil sharpener as he made his way across the room. I could not move a muscle. The man's eyes were glowing red. He had backed me up against the wall before raising the blunt object above his head. I closed my eyes and prepared for impact.

In a moment, when nothing happened, I opened them again. The evil teacher stood frozen with a look of shock upon his face. Mr. Agate then dissipated into the air like a cloud that had been dispersed by a high wind. I sank to my knees and cried grateful tears.

Carlos had successfully destroyed the amulet and saved my life. I owed him everything. The following day, Rose returned to class with her usual sunny know-it-all personality.

Rose remembered nothing of her ordeal. Joy welled up within my heart. I could not take my eyes off of my friends; I was so happy to have them and to be alive.

Weeks later, we were bantering as we always had before class began. I had forgotten to complete my homework. I was stressed out by a number of trivial things and happy to be back under the spell of reality.

A woman walked through the doors of the classroom, dressed sharply in a pinstripe blazer and pencil skirt. Her hair was abnormally smooth and straight, and it almost didn't seem real. She spoke with a steady and reassuring tone. The woman introduced herself to the class as she wrote Ms. Opal across the whiteboard.

❧ 7 ❧

ILL-WILL

I would say that I always knew my best friend Ava was going to get me in trouble, but it is also my fault. I did this to myself and then refused to take responsibility for my actions. I didn't have an angry heart. I took no joy from watching her tear other people apart. I was always afraid that strangers thought that I was the same because I never stopped her.

The truth was, I was so happy to have a friend in this town, that I allowed myself to become silent and awful. I listened to her to make off-color comments to so many people because it makes her feel powerful. I never said a word because I did not want to lose her.

I began slowly seeing all the hurt that I caused. I had always been part of the problem. I knew that I was going to have to walk away from Ava. I didn't want to be alone, with no friends, but it was better than being the worst version of myself.

There was one dark and stormy evening. Ava and I went to see a movie that had just come out in theaters. She talked about her new boyfriend when my thoughts accidentally drifted from the conversation to the sound of the gentle tapping rain on the hood of the car.

Falling raindrops hitting all the different surfaces were among some of my most favorite sounds. It instantly made me feel more comfortable. Even the rolling thunder had a place in my heart. Comfort sounds.

We arrived at the theater and pulled out our umbrellas; Ava walked over to my side and grabbed my arm. I was stuck in a daydream; she didn't like for either of us to cross parking lots alone at night. She had always been protective.

As we were racing to the door, a sad-looking homeless man walked up to us. I hate confrontation or telling people no, so I usually let Ava handle those conversations. She had always been more than willing to take on that task.

"Alice, you can go ahead and buy the tickets. I will be right there," she said. Ava handed me her debit card. I could hear the homeless gentleman softly asking her if she had any change that she could spare.

When I returned to her side, the man appeared to

be crying to himself. I knew that she had said something awful. I knew that I should have told her that speaking to strangers as though they are worthless, makes you a wrong person. I said nothing. I just grabbed her by the arm, and we headed inside to find our seats.

Throughout the show, I thought of his face. The sadness in his eyes. His broken hope. I was so mad at my friend at that moment. I did not want to admit that *I* should have fixed it. I should have said something to him. The only person I am responsible for is me.

When the movie finished, Ava and I took our time exiting the theater. We joked about the storyline of the film we saw and how the actor reminded her of her boyfriend. Everything reminded her of her boyfriend.

Ava stopped dead in her tracks before we walk outside. She looked at me with her eyes widened. She wanted me to beg for information, rather than her just having to tell me outright. I sighed.

"That man! He is still outside, the one I made cry. We need to walk quickly. If he tries to hurt us..." she said.

"Why would he try to hurt us. What did you say to him?" I asked.

"That is not important. What is important is that we leave right this very moment. Maybe we can get a staffer to walk us out to the car," she said.

"I don't think that is necessary," I said. I could not see the man still being upset with her.

The closer we got to the door, the more I realized that the man looked quite a bit different than he had before. He looked put together now; he looked more like a hippy than before too. He was wearing brighter colors now.

A velvet purple scarf hung from his neck. His beard had been cleaned up, and he had on a purple button-up shirt. How did we even tell that was the same man from before when we were so far away?

We passed him quickly and silently. He lifted a solitary finger to point at my friend. I could feel her shuddering where our arms were connected. He was still angry at Ava. What were we to do?

"Come here!" He yelled. My body disobeyed my mind as though he put a spell on me. Ava seemed to be having the same problem. Her feet were moving her closer and closer to the dangerous man, not further away. Soon, we stood shaking in front of him.

"Hello, Girls. My name is simply Test. You may refer to me as Test. You want to know why? This is the fun part... I am a Test," he said. Ava tried to scoff and walk away, but her feet would not move. "That display of selfishness earlier bought you a place on my stage."

"I don't want to play," Ava spat.

"Too bad. I am going to make you play. Feel that?" The man said as he raised a hand in the air. Ava

48

doubled over, holding her hands around her head. Her temples felt like they were going to explode. She finally gave in and agreed to play the game. Tears were rolling down her face. I felt so sorry for her at that moment. Test must have noticed the way I was looking at her.

"Alice. Dear Do-Nothing Alice. I asked your friend for change; she told me that I was better off dead, along with other things. I cried real tears, Alice, because I know she must have said that to someone who was actually in need. She likes to feel powerful, and you are weak and lazy. We are going to see which one of you is the worst!" He said.

"I am going to take everything from you- every last cent. You will live like the people you like to kick around, Ava, unless you solve the riddle. Come back here tomorrow at the same time, with the answer, and I may forgive you. I may spare you. The only issue is that only one of you can be saved. The first one to answer my riddle correctly, will not face The Great Sorrow.

The riddle goes: An impoverished man has this. A rich man desires it. Should you eat it, you will surely die. Bonus points: Ava adds this to Alice's life through her friendship."

"Same time tomorrow?" I confirmed.

"Yes, ma'am. Also, I will make a deal. I don't usually offer so early in, but I am making an exception. If neither of you comes tomorrow, I will split your family's fortunes in half. No one will lose everything. Deal?" He asked.

"Deal," we both replied reluctantly.

Ava and I ran back to the car. She blamed me for not getting a staffer to walk us out. I didn't think it would have made any difference. She seemed needlessly disdainful.

"Neither of us are going tomorrow, right?" I asked.

"Right. We are both staying home tomorrow. There is no need to worry about that man anyway. He is just some entitled creep," Ava said.

I spent the night worrying about my family losing half of their money. We were already pretty broke. I would figure out a way to fix everything. I could get a job and help out just like I had always wanted to. Everything would work out. Splitting the pain was much better than the alternative.

The following day, I went to meet up with Ava at her house. We had plans. Her mom said that she was not home. Ava had told her that she would be with me. I was immediately in denial. I didn't want to believe my eyes and ears.

I hopped in my car and drove to the theater. I saw her already parked among the crowd. Then she opened the door to her vehicle. She was staring dead-ahead at the man in front of her. Test was waiting by the front of the theater.

I followed her up there. When she finally realized

that I was behind her, she sighed. She knew she was going to get caught sooner or later. She had a whole speech prepared.

"I know that this feels like a betrayal, but it isn't. My family has so much money to lose. Half of their fortune would be immense. They would hate me forever," she said.

"What about me? My mother barely makes it from month to month. How could you even rationalize this?" I asked. We were standing in front of the riddle man who looked amused.

"Get a job. You should have one anyway, with your family's expenses. If you just don't answer the riddle, you are going to lose like two hundred dollars. If I ignore it, I lose hundreds of thousands," Ava said.

I sighed. I realized that my friend was too selfish ever to consider anything other than her perspective. I told her to go ahead. Ava nodded her head as though I had made the only correct decision. Ava stood before Test, the riddle man.

"The answer to the riddle is poison. Poor people have poison because of the food they eat. Rich people want poison to take care of their enemies. And if you eat it, you will die. Also, I know that you probably consider me to be poisonous to Alice. It fits in every way. The answer is poison!" Ava said. *Wow.*

"Alice, do you have an answer?" Test asked.

"No, I don't."

"You know that because she already answered, the half contract is void. Do you have an answer now?"

"Yes, I do," I felt myself saying. "The answer is nothing."

Test smiled at me. He placed his hand on mine and told me that I have to pick better friends. I had to be a better person.

Test let Ava weep in the corner before telling us both that he was not taking anyone's wealth. He needed us to learn a lesson. Ava breathed a deep sigh of relief and tried to hug me. I pushed her away.

Test did not take any of her family's money; Ava's father, however, lost half to risky bets. My friend and I went our separate ways, following that incident. I liked Ava still. I could not remain friends with someone who made me worse. There were so many wonderful friends out there who might not put me in that position. I was only going to be looking for people who would not test my morals for no reason.

❧ 8 ❧

SWAMP SISTERS

T he land of the unknown is a great, scary, and sad place. Sometimes the fear and sadness can be cast away when a light is shined upon the darkness. Suddenly the unknown is no longer unknown, and then it can be demystified. Such is the tale of Edwin and the Swamp Sisters.

Edwin fought the scariest spirits, beasts, and ghouls, for a living in the late 1800s. For the right price, the hunter would come to a person's town and get rid of their ghostly pest. Mostly, the souls he freed were angry and full of rage. They stuck around just to make fun of people who might accidentally pass through their territory.

One particular town he was called to, rested on the edge of a dreary swamp. Even he was slightly fearful of wetlands because of their frightening nature. A dense fog hung in the canopy of twisted trees. The dark atmosphere always made him think twice about his job. He found himself fighting his way through swamps more than he cared to admit.

When he arrived in his client's town, he could not help but feel as though the adjacent wetland had infected it. A storm cloud hung above the sad houses. The residents moved around in a sort of haze. They were dressed in rags and remained uncaring about the world around them.

The hunter felt a shiver down his spine. Edwin was not the sort that usually stumbled into this sort of career. He was an intelligent man who happened upon the discovery of monsters quite by accident. Because of an event in his own life, he always vowed to hunt them down. That did not change the fact that his nerves were more likely made from soft lumber than steel.

The town had come together to hire him, or so he had been told. They were all invested in seeing the swamp ghosts disappear. The mayor seemed especially persistent about the matter, flying into a wild rant whenever the subject was discussed.

Edwin paid for his room in town. The innkeeper seemed thrilled for the business. She was a nice older lady whose smile was hiding something. She wanted to tell the ghost hunter a secret, perhaps? Was she too afraid?

Edwin mounted his horse and set off for the cursed swamp beneath the fading light of day. The smell felt like a swift punch to the nose. A strong scent rose up from the murky water, causing the hunter to shake. He was going to have to develop a stronger stomach. He gagged as his horse carefully walked on.

A noise rang out through the dreary dusk, bouncing off the tress. It sounded like a scream; a new smell filled the hunter's nostrils as he ventured deeper into the swamp. Edwin noticed a smokey scent that did not make sense in such a damp place.

He and his horse moved forward through the mushy ground. The earth squished beneath his companion's hooves. Edwin could not help but turn up his nose at the whole scene.

The hunter began to notice shadows moving around from the corner of his eyes. His head would jerk from one side to another, but never with enough speed to catch sight of the entity that seemed to be intentionally bothering him. The thing only motivated Edwin to move more quickly.

That night was forecast to be a full moon, and ghosts could never resist such an event; they always made themselves known. He intentionally chose those evenings so that he might not have to stay in one place for too long. He could find the spirits quickly and then leave.

The air became cold. Edwin listened for sounds, but the entire swampy forest was deadly silent. The drop in temperature was usually a sign that the ghosts were around. He believed that he would find these spirits at any moment now.

The smell of smoke returned. The way to rid one's self of a phantom is to identify its reason for staying attached to our world. You must offer the spirit some sort of compromise. Give it a measure of peace so that it might let go of its earthly attachment. Edwin could sense a ghost near him.

"Save yourself. Leave the town. Danger," a strange voice hissed. Its words seemed to shift from one side of the swamp to the other. Edwin thought about the words it was saying. It sounded less like a threat and more like a warning.

"I am here to help you. I can't do that if I don't know who you are," he said.

The forest seemed to shake around him. It trembled with fear. He looked into the darkness, waiting for a form to appear. A light presented itself in the distance.

There were two of them; the spirits glowed in the darkness of the night as the moon hung high above them. The pair of ghosts moved at the same time as they traversed the Erie land. There was a flow to their motion, a grace. Two such beautiful entities were not what Edwin had been expecting.

The two spirits slowly approached the man. They were lovely. They appeared to be twins. They each had curly brown hair that hung around their shoulders and piercing dark eyes. As they spoke, they passed their words back and forth.

"Fear. Sadness. Pity. Greed. Whatever you must use to rid yourself of the poisonous town, you must go. The swamp birthed evil darkness so long ago, one who ruins the lives of others for fun. You must leave," said the light figures before Edwin.

"I will leave when you let me help you. Tell me why you are here."

"To warn and to protect," they said.

"Why do the townspeople fear you?"

"They do not," said the apparitions.

"Then why am I here? Supposedly hunting you?" Edwin finally asked.

"Who hired you?" They asked. Everyone already knew the answer. "To understand, travel north. Look for the ruins in the clearing. Soon there shall be a road to the next town built right over that land," they said.

Edwin rode his horse to the north. He rode until he found a clearing, which was not far away. He used his lantern to light the area. The spirits sent him to a house that had burnt to the ground.

There were bullet holes and the slash marks from swords mixed in among the rubble. It was as though someone wanted the area completely destroyed. A quiet sadness hung over the land, a sense of mourning; this house was once full of life. It heard laughter, joy, and deep conversations. Then it was mowed down to make way for a road?

Edwin dug inside his saddlebag, looking around for his badge. He pinned it to his jacket and began the long ride back to town. He arrived back in the dark early morning hours. The mayor waited outside of his office for the news. Edwin told him that he would return to him with an update in the morning.

The following day, Edwin sent out several telegrams. He then walked to the mayor's office building and knocked upon the iron door. It creaked open. A sad-looking woman invited him into the building.

The building was the second-largest in town. The inside was fancy, covered with red carpeting. White curtains hung in front of the window. Dark and expensive wood covered the walls and made up the paneling that sectioned off the mayor's office. Glass separated his highness from the rest of the world.

The mayor came running in a lively manner with a smile stretched across his chubby cheeks. He was wearing a suit made of beautiful royal blue fabric.

"I trust that you have rid of us these pests?" He asked Edwin.

"I am about to rid your entire town of the only

pest," said Edwin. The mayor looked at the hunter with an expression of confusion.

"Well, get to it, I guess. I thought that you would have our problem sorted by now. You went on a long ride into the forest yesterday, did you not?" He asked.

"Indeed, I did. For research. Sir, do you know how to rid yourself of a phantom? I suspect not, so allow me to tell you. One must first identify the spirit and what they want. Then you must give it to them. Offer the ghosts something of a solution to their issues, so that they are no longer forced to attach to the living world," said Edwin.

"Well, I trust that you'll have the issue worked out with some speed, then. Good day," said the mayor.

"Not so quick, sir. I have worked out the issue. You are under arrest, sir," said the hunter.

"What!? That is silly. Why ever would you think my arrest could solve our issue. You have no authority," said the frightened mayor.

"The spirits lurk about this land because you took their lives and their home to build a road. They told me as much. I suspect that you are also taxing your town dry," said Edwin. "I have received permission from the federal level, and I am to bring you to headquarters. I would not dare go about my job without being deputized, sir."

And as the mayor was taken away, the rain cloud

over the sad swampy town dissolved. The people all stared and grinned as their former mayor was being walked through town. Perhaps, even the ghosts that haunted the wetlands smiled that day, before they vanished into the damp air.

❋ 9 ❋

SPELLING BEE

The young witches, magicians, and wizards practiced their magic in secret. Telling anyone about their gift could mean trouble for their families. No mortal in town knew about the abilities of their neighbors.

The king had decided a long time ago, that magic was not allowed within the kingdom. Anyone found using powers would be kicked out of the realm and left to take care of themselves. No among of danger could keep any of the students from practicing. Each night, the children and their parents would sneak out to the forest beneath the cover of darkness.

Every student was different. They had all inherited their talents through their family. Their special powers always showed themselves in time. Some of the were still waiting for their first sign of magic. It bloomed like a flower when the time was right.

Those who did not yet have their gifts would still travel out to the woods, just like the rest. For a few hours every night, they would try to make their magic appear. There were so many different methods to use when practicing. Some used their emotions. Others used relaxation to focus their energy.

Abby was already a powerful witch. She found her powers at a very early age. She was able to change objects into entirely different things. She had one of the most impressive gifts in the entire land.

The young lady first noticed her abilities when she was a child. She focused on a flower, accidentally turning it into a toad. The animal croaked and then hopped away from her. Abby was amazed that she was about to accomplish something so incredible. No other witch had ever done anything like that before; she was the first.

There was only one issue with witches; they were the most competitive of all the magical beings. No amount of power was enough for any of them. Each witch wanted to be the best. They were all made with a desire to succeed, built-in.

Magicians and wizards were more laid back and often avoided engaging with the witches during their games and competitions. They were too powerful. They were too dangerous.

Abby was drawn into this drive to be the best. She believed that she knew more than anyone else. She would not take advice or guidance from a single soul, not even her grandmother.

Abby's grandmother had been an amazingly powerful witch in her prime. She could change the shape or color of subjects. She had offered to teach Abby all about her gifts and how she used them. The young girl had refused the woman's guidance.

With great sadness, her grandmother left town. She could not bear to see Abby going down such a dark path. Angry words were spoken between Abby and her grandmother.

Abby felt as though her grandmother was trying to dethrone her. She was paranoid about everyone she met. The fear she felt made her dangerous.

One particular night, all of the magical beings were practicing their gifts in the forest. The woodlands were bathed in the light of the moon; darkness consumed the rest of the world. A young and ambitious witch named Hannah challenged Abby to a competition. They would use their abilities to decide who was more competent with magic. Abby declined, determined not to involve herself in petty squabbles. Hannah mocked and taunted so she would relent, and the pair could have their battle.

"Wow, just like I thought. You can't live up to your grandmother's powers!" Said Hannah. She was trying to get under Abby's skin, and it worked. Abby's eyes filled with rage.

The pair lined up for their contest. Abby and

Hannah were both supposed to showcase their magic against a stick from the forest floor. Powers were never allowed to be turned against one another, for any reason.

Abby understood the rules but somehow believed herself to be above them. Abby told herself that she was so powerful, there was no way she could hurt another contestant without intending to do so. She believed she had too much control over her magic.

Most of the other witches, wizards and magicians gathered around the pair, to watch. Abby's parents joined the crowd. They all stood in a circular clearing. The moon shone down upon the group as the contest was about to start.

Hannah went first. Her stick grew roots and planted itself in the ground, becoming a huge tree. Leaves bloomed from the fresh branches as the trunk continued upward. The entire crowd was amazed. They all clapped and cheered for the young witch. Abby felt her face becoming hot.

Abby had an idea. She would prove herself by using her grandmother's powers against Hannah. Abby would turn her blue for a few hours. She had never attempted such a task before, but she was confident she could do it.

The young witch closed her eyes and focused her mind. She imagined her opponent in her mind, envisioning Hannah changing colors. She opened her eyes to see nothing happening. Abby had to pretend to focus on the stick. No one could know that she was going to embarrass Hannah.

Abby tried again. She pushed all of her emotions forward and readied herself. Something buzzed by her head, the young witch opened her eyes to see (what she believed was) an angry bee lunging toward her. She lost her focus and began to swat at the insect.

The forest was silent, except for buzzing. Abby looked all around herself. She had turned the entire crowd to bees, including her parents. Her heart sank.

Abby began to panic; she had never felt such fear. She had no idea what to do to fix the mess. The young witch began to sob as she thought of her parents being trapped in the bodies of bees forever. There was nothing that she could do.

She screamed out into the night, even though that was dangerous. If the village heard her, she'd be kicked out of the kingdom. Abby could not stop crying.

The handful of witches, magicians, and wizards, who had gone off on their own and missed the contest appeared from the forest. Abby cried as she explained what happened. The bees were going off in different directions. She was going to lose them all soon.

A wizard named Sally hugged Abby. She tried her best to comfort the young witch, even though they had never spoken before that moment. Sally was the sweetest magical being in the realm. She was compassionate and caring to a fault.

Sally had not yet discovered her magic. She had no idea that her compassion and kindness were connected to her powers. She hugged the crying witch, trying to calm her.

Where Sally's hands touched Abby's back, she felt warmth. Her back tingled. Something was happening. Something *magical*.

All around the witches, wizards, and magicians, thuds were heard coming from the forest. It was the sound of human bodies dropping to the forest floor. Sally had reversed the spell!

Abby cried happy tears as her angry friends and family made their way back to the clearing. She apologized for the mess she made. The runaway spell had offered her humility.

Abby conceded that Hannah won the game. She apologized to Hannah again. Abby hugged her parents and began to gather her things.

"Honey, where are you going!? It's dark out. Are you going home?" Abby's mother called out.

"No, mom. There is someone I have to go see," Abby said. The young witched smiled. She set out upon the path to her grandmother's house.

❧ 10 ❧

SOCKS

My grandmother steadied herself using my arm as we walked along in search of the mysterious wishing well. I had read about the place online, and she remembered visiting it from her childhood. There was a legend that states that one in a million wishes were granted.

The well was hidden deep within a forest that no one walks any longer. Many decades ago, there was a trail that cut right through the heart of it. Parents brought their children for a nice jog down the path.

Since it was let go, I had expected the area to be overgrown. The walking path was still obvious. My grandmother decided that meant there was still magic in the woodlands. I decided that it meant there was a secret admirer of old hiking trials somewhere out there.

The hike featured some of the most beautiful and calming natural scenes. Relaxing streams flowed around the forest floor. Animals ran around through streamers of daylight that fought their way through patches of leaves in the canopy.

Birds chirped a chipper song. It was perhaps a little random, but still lovely. There was even a soft wind that gently blew against our skin as we walked along. I was just pleased to have such quality time with my grandmother. She was brilliant and hilarious.

She also remembered where all the coolest spots in town were, including this wishing well. I brought one coin, as not to cheat the system. I wondered how much metal now lay at the bottom of this mysterious hole in the ground.

We arrived at a circular clearing, in the center was a stone well. I had assumed that it would be in a state of disrepair, but it was perfect. There was even a beautiful stone roof/canopy covering the opening, complete with a wooden bucket.

"I am going to wish for something crazy," I said.

"Be careful, Ethan, magic is serious business," she warned.

"How else will I know that it worked?" I asked, laughing.

"Wish for happiness or something, honey," she replied.

"See, that is a boring wish. Besides, didn't you say

something about balance? If I magically do well, doesn't that mean that someone else will have to fail magically?" I asked.

"You are right, Ethan. It is perhaps best not to wish at all. Or maybe think of something small and safe. I used to wish for a delicious birthday cake, but I also wasn't the brightest child," she said.

"Fine! I wish for an unconditional wish!"

"I don't think the universe works that way," my grandmother said. She tried not to laugh at the absurdity of our conversation.

"Okay, I got it. I will wish for the first thing that comes to mind as I toss the coin in. Something truly spontaneous!" I raised my penny high in the air and then flipped it down into the well. I smiled to myself. She followed suit, tossing her own into the well.

"Well? What did you wish for?" She asked after the moment passed.

"I don't think I am supposed to tell you. Look at it this way though, if it comes true then you will surely know," I said. She looked both amused and concerned. We started making our way down the path back to the car.

She dropped me back off at my house, and I hugged her. When I opened the door, my mother called for me from the kitchen. I threw my coat onto a chair and followed her voice back.

The legs of the chairs at our kitchen table make

an awful sound when they are drug out. I winced from the screech and took a seat to chat with my mom as she cooked diner. She was an adorably short lady with wavy dark hair that she fought to keep out of her face.

My cat, Socks, jumped into my lap. My mom scolded me for allowing him near the table, so I pushed him to the ground. He huffed and stalked away.

Mom asked about my wish, and I refused to tell her anything. I remember noting how seriously my family took all that superstition. Ella, our dog, sat on the ground in front of me. She was begging because she thought I had food. I waved her away. We had two dogs and a cat; I liked the cat a lot more.

The night went on like a thousand nights before it had done. We ate, went about our separate business, and then I went to bed. The day we'd spent hiking had exhausted me. I tossed and turned all night, having the weirdest dreams.

I awoke to the face of a stranger staring at me. I froze, completely unable to move or scream. The stranger seemed confused by my horror. Thinking quickly, I grabbed my alarm clock and threw it at his face as hard as possible. He shrieked and hit me with a closed fist.

I held my aching eye. That is when I noticed that he was wearing my clothing, with my right eye. There was something familiar about his face, but I could not put my finger on it. We were both in pain now, just sitting and looking at one another.

"I am the cat. I am not sure how I can speak English. I thought that would be an issue, but here we are. I guess I have a human brain now, too," said the stranger. He appeared to be roughly my age with black hair and pale skin. Socks was a white cat with a few inky splotches. This intruder was pretty much a correct representation if he were to be changed into human form. I could not help but laugh hysterically. That had to be a joke. One of them correctly guessed my wish and...

A scream rang out from downstairs. My mom had discovered the dogs turned people. Ella was a plump blonde woman with a sweet face; she had large eyes and a small dainty mouth. She was wearing my father's clothing because my mother had a petit frame. Axel (our other former dog) sat beside Ella, on the couch. He looked like a college frat boy that had lived his life as a golden retriever before enrolling. And he had, so I guess that is accurate.

My family had a long conversation about my wish from the day before and how it was irresponsible of me to play with magic. Socks came to my defense, saying that he enjoyed being a human. Mom said that they couldn't support such a large household. I thought she was going to throw them out, but she just stated that they would all need to look for work after they had adjusted to the change.

Everyone got along really well. There were even some healing talks associated with certain parties having been told to stay away from the furniture or keep off the table. My mom had to hear some harsh truths, but she took it like a champ.

The first day was a dream. Socks was going to be such a fun friend to have. I was excited to show him everything he had been missing. I found out that he wants to be allowed to roam outside. I had never even thought of allowing him out. I was also in a unique position to explain cars and roads to him while he can understand.

I slept on the floor to allow him to experience sleeping in a bed. I awoke with Socks staring at me again. I screamed before my brain realized that I was not in danger.

"Rule number one to being human: do NOT watch people while they sleep. It's unsettling," I said.

"You look strange, that's all," said Socks. My mother screamed from downstairs. I looked into my mirror to see that I had tall triangular ears appearing on the top of my head. My skin was covered in a light layer of hair. My heart fell into my stomach as I looked over the changes. I could have cried. I was turning into a cat.

My mother called everyone to the living room. She begged me to tell her that the change was not permanent. She had floppy ears and a snout. My father had similar features.

"I don't know. I don't see why the changes wouldn't be permanent," I said.

"We have to find a way to fix this!" She replied.

"Now, hang on a minute, everyone. What if it is permanent? We all know what pets need already. We can take good care of you. Its' our turn to be human," said Axel. I laughed and looked to Socks to see if he found that amusing too. He did not.

"I agree with the dog. You guys have been human your entire lives. It's genuinely unfair. Who knows if you will even turn entirely into cats or dogs? If you do, I assure you that I don't mind if you sit on the kitchen table," Socks said.

"I am sorry that I told you to get down. Please don't use that as a reason to condemn me forever," mom said.

"Condemn to what, living our lives? I would sentence you to that in a flash," said Socks. Everyone in the room became silent. The dogs looked guilty, but they refused to speak.

"Did you not like living with us?" I said, finally.

"It's not that. It's just that humans are so free. I don't feel guilty for wanting my freedom. I will fight you for it; it's nothing personal. I want to be able to eat what I want when I want. I want to sit where I want and play when I want. Look on the bright side; if you change completely into animals, then you won't know freedom exists, and you will be happy," said Socks.

The house was suddenly filled with tension. I could tell my mother was seriously considering asking the animal-humans to leave, but then we would be on our own. That could be disastrous if the change was permanent or if we continued morphing into pets. We all broke off on our own. I locked myself inside my room and sobbed for a while. I was such a stupid boy. What a stupid wish; I was stuck in a nightmare.

As the hours wore on, I kept changing. I was slowly losing my thumbs. My body was beginning to shrink, and I began to panic. I didn't know what else to do. I made a call and then turned on the television and tried to escape my doom for a while.

That night, I hugged my parents tightly. We all cried. We were going to keep changing during the night, and who knows when I would be able to hug my parents again. Or if I would even know that they were my parents.

The following day, I awoke in the body of a cat. I still had my brain and my thoughts. Colors were weird and muted. It was as though someone placed an awful online photo filter over all of reality. I couldn't speak; the only sounds I made were always a variant of "meow."

Socks picked me up and placed me on the bed. He had somehow gotten into my room during the night.

Thank goodness, I would have been trapped. He tried to calm me, but I was hysterical. The guy-cat had the nerve to tell me that things were better this way. I disagreed.

The following day was one of the worst of my life because I was trapped inside something else's body. I ate cat food (gross) and purred involuntarily. I had to witness my parents suffering in the same enteral prison, because of me and my stupid wish.

I went to sleep with no hope. I rested curled in a ball on the floor. On the bright side, the brain decline was setting in. I was having a difficult time remembering things and then thinking in general. I was more concerned with the present moment than with more profound thought.

I woke up the next day with an awful pain in my back. I opened my eyes to find Socks angrily staring at me. Fur covered his face. He was in the in-between. So was I!

I called my grandmother the day before and begged her to help. She told me she would figure something out. I did not expect it to work; I thought we were all doomed. I ran downstairs and immediately hugged my parents.

I found out that she took ten thousand dollars from her savings and made a million wishes. It took her all day and all night, but her plan worked. Before Socks turned back into a cat, I asked him or information about what I could do to be a better companion for him. He was mad but eventually calmed enough to give me a list.

The next day, everything returned to normal. Mother was cooking dinner, and I sat at the dining room table. We chatted as she worked. Socks sat on the table in front of me, wagging his tail.

11

SEWER GOBLINS

J essica lived in a small town. She and her best
friend Lacey passed their time by exploring
new areas. The friends would often go out in
search of adventures; that was their favorite
activity.

They'd spent all summer making their fun. The
pair began going to a public pool. There was always a
large crowd enjoying the cold water, escaping the
heat. Jessica loved the diving board.

Even though the pool was becoming more
popular among the locals, Jessica and Lacey still had
fun. They also managed to make some new friends.
Two sisters, named Cassie and Kim, began to hang
out with the girls often.

The sisters were a lot more rebellious than Jessica
and Lacey. They were always getting into trouble for
their adventures. They had a dangerous streak. Lacey

admitted that she thought they were exciting and fun but also a little scary. The sisters just were not afraid of anything.

It was one warm day at the pool, that fate set her plans into motion. The friends were all sitting on their towels, trying to dry off beneath the midday sun. A light breeze cooled their skin. Lacey took this chance to reapply sunscreen, while Jessica chatted with the newest additions to their small group.

The moment Jessica told the sisters that she and Lacey enjoyed exploring, their eyes lit up. Lacey's eyes widened. She knew, at that moment, that her friend had made a mistake.

"We need to go find some new places, then! I know of a place that I think you guys will love," Cassie said.

"Where is it?" Asked Lacey, looking a little nervous. The sisters looked at one another, laughing as though it were an inside joke.

"It is a secret, but you will love it," said Kim.

"Well, it will have to wait a day. I'm going to work with my mom tomorrow. Bring Your Child to Work Day. I can't get out of it," said Jessica. She was more excited to find out the secret than her friend.

"Where does your mom work?" Asked Kim.

"The library. It's in that huge old building, downtown," said Jessica.

"That place is creepy looking! It's ancient," said Kim. Jessica laughed; she had once felt the same way.

"Mom said that the place was constructed in the 1800s," said Jessica. The brick building was huge, with so many rooms and hallways. They were all filled with books (as you might expect). There was something mysterious about the place that always fascinated Jessica. Fancy seals were carved into every wooden doorway. The details in those images were terrific; it consisted of a large tree with open books and other symbols on either side.

The girls spent the rest of their time at the pool, telling stories about the most frightening places that they had visited. These tales were so funny because everything was scary to Lacey. She mentioned the time she was lost in a grocery store when she was a child, then a mean dog in a local park.

The next day, Jessica followed her mom around at work. Her mother had always been reluctant about her job. It could be hard work to get any details out of the woman at home. They both loved *Bring Your Child to Work Day*, though.

Jessica was fascinated by the library; there was so much information in one building. It was such a silent and calming environment and one full of mystery. Their days together always passed too quickly.

Jessica woke up the next morning to the sound of her alarm clock. She quickly shot up and got dressed because it was going to be a wonderful day. The sisters were going to take Jessica and Lacey to their secret spot.

Jessica met Lacey in the park between their houses. The weather was perfect! A glowing summer sun beat down upon the girls, but the wind cooled them. Trees in the area were all such lovely shades of green. There seemed to be an electricity in the air.

Lacey looked more worried than excited. She was staring off into space when Kim and Cassie arrived. One of the sisters carried a backpack and dressed as though they were ready for a hike.

"We are going to be walking through a forest nearby. I've been there hundreds of times, so there is nothing to be scared of, Lacey. You guys can just follow us," said Kim. And so, the adventure began.

The forest looked so full and lively. Animals scampered away as the four girls passed through. Leaves crunched beneath the shoes of the friends, constantly giving away the location of the group, to deer and squirrels. It did not seem as though they were following any path; they were all walking around trees and bushes.

The ground was hilly and included the occasional creek. Soon, the girls found themselves walking beside a small stony cliff. Cassie and Kim seemed to be looking for this landmark, and it didn't take long to understand why.

Up ahead, Jessica saw the mouth of a cave. She and Lacey both gasped at the sight. She had never seen a cave in person before. Kim and Cassie insisted that they all enter the cavern.

"There is a long hallway inside. It is so cool. There is a door at the end that won't open. We aren't sure what it connects to," said Kim.

The sisters brought a flashlight to lead the way. The inside of the cave was dark, chilly, and damp. Dripping was heard coming from somewhere. From the ceiling hung ice sickles that looked like stone or gems.

Lacey grabbed Jessica's arm to steady herself. The darkness scared Lacey, as did being inside of a cave. She remained silent, trying not to mess up the fun for anyone else. Lacey would one day learn to trust her gut.

Finally, the friends came to the closed stone door. There were symbols carved into the rock that seemed familiar to Jessica. She could not place where she had seen the signs before.

Each of the girls tried to push the door. They didn't want to open it, but they wanted to see if it would move. It did not budge.

Then, Jessica noticed something shiny embedded in the cavern wall. Whenever the flashlight was passed over the object, it lit up. Curiosity got the better of Jessica as she walked over and touched it.

The small shining object was a button made of red gemstone. She pointed it out of the rest of her friends. Kim and Cassie told her to press it, but Jessica refused. She felt uneasy about the situation.

The sisters pushed her out of the way and pressed the button themselves. It took a lot of force to move down. Nothing happened, and Lacey breathed a sigh of relief. She had been so scared something awful would happen.

Then the entire cave began to shake. A loud and frightening sound came from behind the stone door, as though something was growling. The door flew open. Lacey grabbed her friend's hand, and they stood perfectly still against the wall of the cavern. The sisters did the same on the opposite side.

Suddenly, there was a stampede of disgusting creatures. They ran on their back legs while dragging their hands against the ground like monkeys. They were thin and dark green. The flashlight had fallen on the ground. One of the creatures picked it up and examined it.

The fallen light illuminated a portion of the ground, the girls to see the long fangs and glowing yellow eyes of the creature. The beast's skin was patchy and peeling in some places. The monster shrieked as it threw the flashlight down and continued running. The smell of sewage filled the noses of the terrified girls. They had yet to be spotted by the evil creatures.

The "animals" screamed as they ran out into the daylight. The sound was unsettling and loud. When the last one had exited the cave, the girls took a few moments to recover from the excitement. Lacey was crying. Jessica's mouth was still hung open.

The sisters were the first to move. No one said a word. No one knew what had just happened, and they all felt crazy. Jessica stepped forward to pick up the flashlight. That is when she realized where she had recognized the symbols on the stone door.

She told her friends to follow her. The girls all ran as fast as they could. One of the creatures spotted the friends; it chased them through the forest before giving up. Lacey slipped, and Jessica doubled back, grabbing her friend's arm and yanking her to her feet just in time. She could feel the monster's breath against her face.

The girls finally outran the creature. Jessica had led them straight to the library. She rushed inside the building with her friends behind her. Jessica broke down crying when she saw her mother. She could not hold the emotion in any longer.

When Jessica had calmed down, she told her mom what had happened. Her friends just listened in silence. Lacey was still shaking. None of them expected the woman to believe the story, but Jessica thought it was worth a shot.

"I know that you probably don't believe a word of this, mom. I am so sorry. I can't believe any of this either," Jessica said when she finished the story.

"I believe you," said her mother.

"What? Why?" Asked Jessica.

"Because I know the creatures you describe. They are called Sewer Goblins. We should have sealed the cave better. Whoever had the idea that the door to the cave should open with the push of a button, should be fired!" Jessica's mother said. The girls all stood there, shocked. "This is more than just a library. We keep the town safe from things like Sewer Goblins. We are going to take care of this," she added.

"Can I come?" Asked Jessica, still stunned.

"Not yet, little one," she said. Jessica's mother then turned to an unassuming coworker in a floral dress. The woman had tiny glasses resting on the bridge of her nose. "Gladys! Suit up! The Sewer Goblins are out again." Gladys rolled her eyes and laughed as she picked up a suitcase from behind the checkout desk.

12

THE IDEAL MATE

There was a small table by the window at a café in Hapeville. From the hours of five to six p.m., that seat stayed empty for Misti. The owners watched the same young lady come into their building, day after day. They liked her. She was polite to the staff and a little goofy.

Mitsi had been coming into the Dreaming Bean for as long as she could remember. It was her escape from the outside world. Her father was a politician, so life at home was full of drama.

There was always some bill that he had voted poorly on or some law that he opposed. Reporters surrounded her and her family, still, but somehow, they did not know about the Dreaming Bean. Here, she was just like any other young lady. Her life outside of the café was lonely and sad.

Mitsi would never tell a soul, but she hated the

taste of the coffee. It made her face scrunch up. She bought a cup every single day. No one ever noticed that she never took a sip. Instead, it was the smell that she loved. It was cozy. She loved hanging her head over the steaming cup while she worked, or pretended to work, or daydreamed.

There was one more secret that Mitsi would never share. She, more than anything, wanted a friend. She longed for company or someone with whom to talk. The young lady showed up to the Dreaming Bean every day, hoping she would meet someone else like her. She had developed a hopeless crush on one of the staffers who served her the fake coffee on most of her trips. His name was Pat. Mitsi's life was lonely.

It seemed as though the loneliness was only going to get worse. There were rumors that Mitsi's father was involved in an illegal scam of some sort. The news had not touched her life yet, but she could see the wave headed her way. The worst part? She didn't know if her dad was guilty or innocent.

Mitsi held her cup close to her nose, calming her nerves with the steam. There were strange people in the café that day. They'd been coming for a week. A whole team of very serious businessmen sitting at a table in the corner who just watched the customers as they came and went. She hoped that they weren't there for her because of her father.

The following day, a handsome stranger bought

CAMPFIRE STORIES FOR KIDS: A SCARY GHOST, WITCH, AN...

her coffee for her. He asked to sit at her table. Mitsi was a shy young lady, but she agreed. His name was Aaron, he said. He was so easy to talk to, she almost forgot who she was.

He had a perfectly chiseled face and a welcoming smile. Misti would have gotten lost in his eyes if they weren't just a little weird. Aaron's eyes were a bright and almost unnatural blue color.

Aaron immediately became a regular. He sat with Mitsi every day, talking about her interests. Somehow, they liked all of the same things. She found herself telling him everything about her life.

The stranger was everything she had been looking for, but something about him was off. She thought that maybe she was being silly. She should feel over-the-moon happy. *Perhaps I just feel weird because it's all just happening so fast,* she thought.

Aaron and Mitsi eventually became a couple. If she had made any friends, they would have been jealous. He was nearly perfect; he was intelligent, handsome, and funny.

The young man was soon invited to her family's house for dinner, at his insistence. She hadn't wanted him to know about her father, but there was no way to keep it a secret forever. Aaron got along so well with her family; her father loved him.

The pair chatted for a whole hour while she and her mother cleaned up the dishes. Mitsi heard thundering laughter from her father's den. She was happy that the night was going so well.

Aaron became a little distant following the dinner date. He made excuses for reasons why he could not see Mitsi, for days at a time. The young woman felt like she should have been sadder about his coldness, but she was not.

One day, the family's security guard called Mitsi into the room with the monitors from all the cameras. What he showed her, chilled her to the bone. She had never been more afraid in her life.

Every single night, eighteen minutes of security footage went missing. The guard had noticed and planted extra cameras around the outside of the house. Finally, he caught the person responsible.

Aaron stood deathly still, outside of her parent's house for precisely eighteen minutes. He did not move an inch. Mitsi thought she was going crazy, but it looked like his eyes were also glowing in the darkness.

Is he getting information on my father? Is he a stalker? An alien? Is he going to hurt me? What do I do?

Mitsi's thoughts were running wild. She decided that there was nothing to do other than break up with him. The young woman was shaking with fear.

The following day, at the Dreaming Bean, she tried to let him down easy. Aaron looked hurt. Or like he was trying to look hurt but had never seen a sad person before. He demanded that she give him a second chance.

Mitsi said that she could not but did not tell him why. She didn't want him to hurt her, and she was afraid he might. She was still shaking, which he noticed. Her favorite staffer, Pat, brought her coffee to their table. He watched Aaron for a moment before going back to the counter.

That night, upon leaving the café, he followed her. Her mind kept running over the worst possible reasons. She stopped on a sidewalk and yelled for him to leave her alone. He finally turned and walked in the other direction. Misty breathed a sigh of relief.

The following day rain poured down all day. Despite the intense weather, Mitsi had neither seen nor heard from Aaron. His absence gave her room to breathe and a chance to sigh with relief.

"So, uh... I have a weird question," said a voice from behind Mitsi. Pat took a seat at her table. He looked worried. "Have you ever seen him in the rain?"

"Who?" Mitsi asked, playing dumb.

"The man. Have you ever seen him when it's raining outside? I have never seen him out when it's raining. I thought maybe I was going crazy," Pat said. "I noticed that he was a little scary toward you yesterday, can I make a suggestion?" Mitsi was still confused about his first sentence.

"Sure," she said.

"If he bothers you again, spill your coffee on him.

I don't even know if it will work or if I am losing my mind. I can bring you room temperature coffee. I could even bring water in a coffee cup. Just, if he shows up again... accidentally spill a little on him. I am sorry. I have to get back to work," Pat said.

That was the strangest conversation that Mitsi had ever taken part in if you could call it that. She could not stop thinking about Pat's words. *What could they mean?*

The following day, Aaron showed up to the café again. He sat with Mitsi and placed his hand upon her arm. Aaron gazed through her with his strange eyes and began laying out a story about why he had been acting so weird. He said he hadn't meant to scare her when he followed her.

Mitsi signaled for Pat to bring her the drink. When he sat it down, he very obviously announced to the table that he brought her the usual coffee. She thanked him, and then he went back to his counter and watched their table.

Mitsi sighed, trying to gather her courage. She slipped the lid of the cup up with her finger and then "accidentally" pushed the liquid all over Aaron. He looked surprised at first.

"I am so sorry. I can't believe I did that," Mitsi said.

"He brought you water when you ordered a coffee," Aaron said. Mitsi opened her mouth. She was going to respond. Before she could say a word, sparks started coming from Aaron.

His head began to flick back and forth. Aaron's eyes turned black and then back to blue and then black again. Instead of words, he was making the sounds CDs do when they skip. More sparks flew from him, and his arm caught fire. Mitsi saw the metal beneath his new suit.

Two men burst through the front door of the café, as Mitsi watched in horror. They used towels to put the fire out. The men picked up their glitching robot and hauled him out of the café.

Every person inside the Dreaming Bean turned their attention to Mitsi. She could only shrug. She did not know what else she could do.

"How on earth did you know?" Mitsi asked Pat weeks later, on their first date.

"He was extraordinarily strange and mechanical. I thought I might be going insane for thinking it, but then, I am pretty sure that I saw him plug himself into the wall with a phone charging cord."

13

THE GHOSTS IN WENDELL FOREST

Wendell has always had ghosts. That is not a secret in our town. We discourage newcomers because we know that the spirits can be hard to handle. The townspeople here have made up all sorts of lies to keep people from moving here.

This past summer, I made friends with a boy whose family moved here. His name was Nick; he was my age. My mom tried so hard to keep me from hanging out with him.

"Gus, you know that his family isn't going to stay here. They are going to have to leave. Those are the rules. They are going to find a way to run his family out of town," she said.

I pushed my hair out of my face so that I could better glare at my mother. I knew that the town was going to try to force his family out. I just wanted a friend. We had gotten along so well. We liked all of the same movies and found all of the same jokes funny.

"Gus," she said, as though she were reading my mind, "one day you will have more friends. Don't make friends with people who are only going to be here for a second. It's only going to hurt you."

Then again, I knew something that she didn't know. Nick's father was a famously tough lawyer. The family was probably not going to run from their new house without a fight.

We are not allowed to talk about the spirits to anyone from out of town. I planned on breaking that rule. I was on my way to break it. I left the house, telling mom that I was going to the store for a school project.

I knocked at Nick's front door as I listened intently for the sound of footsteps inside the house. His father answered, looking upset; the town must have already begun their work. The attorney ran his hand through his hair and told me to come in. I was jealous of my friend for having the coolest father. He was so easy to speak to, but I guess that's because he was a lawyer. As if on cue, Nick's father asked me to sit while I waited on him.

"Any idea why everyone in town is scowling at me? They have disconnected my light bill for the third time this week, and someone is firing gunshots outside of the house at night. I don't know what to think of this place, Gus. I am sorry that I am telling you all this, you are a kid," the man said. There was so much confusion in his eyes that I decided then that I was going to explain it to him too.

"I will tell you, Mr. Reid, but you're going to think I am losing my mind," I said. He looked interested.

"No, please. I promise not to judge you. I want to know why I am treated like a second-class citizen. I think someone keyed my car yesterday," he said.

Nick came downstairs, asking if I was ready to go. His father motioned for the young man to join our conversation. He sat beside me on their couch.

"Gus is going to explain the awful behavior of the town. He is going to tell me what I did," he said. I laughed, thinking that Mr. Reid was joking. He was not.

"It isn't personal. Look, Wendell had always had issues. The locals are mean to those who move here or try to because they want to protect others from having to deal with the same issues. The issues can physically hurt you if you don't know how to handle them. Wendell is a dangerous place. I don't want you guys to leave, though," I said. I realized how selfish I was being, right after I said it.

"Gus. What? You're trying to tell me that they are mean because they like us?" Nick asked.

"No, they don't attach to you or anyone else. It's about saving as many families as we are able. I am just going to say it; we have a ghost problem. They are everywhere. The forest is full of spirits, and the houses and streets also have their fair share," I said. Nick and his father both began to laugh. He realized that I was not joking and tried to hold the sounds inside.

"I can prove it. I will go with you to the forest after dark, and you will understand," I said. Nick's father didn't say anything for a while. He was probably thinking about how cruel it would be to let me continue to believe my delusions. After some begging, they agreed.

I returned to my house and lied again about my whereabouts. Mom would have a heart attack if she knew that I was going to the haunted forest. I filled three heavy-duty squirt guns with lemon juice because acidic liquids make the ghosts disperse. Those two items are always sold out in town.

We headed toward the woods. The path through town was abnormally calm. It was as though the spirits knew I wanted them to show up for once. The streets were utterly empty of people too. The ghosts always came out at night, so maybe I should have waited for the sun to go down. It would be dark by the time we got to the forest.

Immediately, upon stepping past the tree line, we heard noises. The wind rustled through the branches above us. I put out my arm to stop them from moving. Nick's father laughed at himself for being caught up in the moment and believing me for just an instance. I flipped on the flashlight.

"Gus, animals live in the forest," he said.

A pure white light figure with pitch-black eyes appeared and screamed in his face. I sprayed it with my squirt gun, and it dissolved back into the air. Nick screamed. His father was about to start asking questions, but there was no time in between attacks.

A solid looking black blob was floating toward us. I would not have seen it without my flashlight. The dark blobs are especially evil stained souls, they say. My friend was frozen in place, watching the monsters as they advanced. I had only known that fear when I was very young. I was born into this weirdness.

I pulled them back out in the direction that we came. Nick looked as though he were unable to speak. They were now visible all over the fields beside the town. And in the streets of the town. They were everywhere.

"W-w-why?" Asked the lawyer.

"That is a difficult question. I will tell you what I have always heard. The story goes that Wendell is a supernatural haven of sorts. Or it was. Not ghosts or spirits, but beasts and monsters were once thought to roam the forest. They took people from the community, one by one. There was nowhere else our ancestors could go; they were trapped in Wendell. Fanged monsters terrorized and frightened people for fun.

"So, one day, all the witches in town banded

together. They cast a spell to form a shield of human spirits over the town. Essentially, the same people who cast the spell are the ones protecting us now. We are safe from all kinds of attacks, especially those of a supernatural nature. The trade-off is ghosts," I said.

"Then why-" said Nick's father.

"Why do they attack? Because they are all different. Some of them are angry. Some are wise. Some of them are aimlessly wandering. Others lash out at anything that moves. Listen, I know that Wendell has some quirks..." They both laughed. "I know that there are some issues here, but think about staying. The town had a lot to offer. The woods are beautiful in daylight!" I said.

❧ 14 ❧
CART OF DARKNESS

I have seen the ugliest parts of this world. There is more darkness than any simple words could describe; I would need something more intense.

There are places on this planet where no man should venture. They only exist to inflict pain and suffering. I learned this lesson when I was just a child. Sometimes I wonder if the experience made me crazy. Allow me to tell you about the worst place I have ever seen.

There was a grocery store called Deals and Saves. This thing had so many aisles, and when I was seven, they towered above me. I loved going shopping with my mother to any other store but this one.

I was riding on the bottom of my mother's cart one day. I had fallen asleep against the gate part that connects to the wheels. I must have rolled off at some point. As I fell to the ground, I yelled for my mother, but she could not hear me. She was too far away. I picked myself up and ran to catch up to her.

I rounded the corner, and she was no longer there. There was only an army of other shoppers who were all angry with me for getting in their way. I didn't know what to do, so I just kept walking.

I heard a huge roar coming up behind me. I turn to see a massive machine that looks as though it is going to run me over. The sound that it makes thunders out through the store.

The machine is gray and full. Two blade-like attachments spun around the bottom. The man driving it looked downright evil. I knew that he was after me. I knew that he was going to eat me alive with the horrible monster.

I began to run. It seemed as though I was running forever. There was no sight of my mother. Strangers were giving me angry looks as I tried to pass them. A woman in a different machine almost ran me over. They all seemed to be trying to hit me. I had done something wrong, and now I must pay.

The aisles went on forever. There was always one more to walk through. I became frightened, and I began to shake. I sat down in the middle of the floor, and a woman immediately hit me in the head with her cart. I ran again, tears falling from my eyes.

A booming voice came from the loudspeaker,

thanking me for shopping at Deals and Saves. I covered my ears and slowed my pace to a walk. Finally, there was a light in the darkness. A nice old lady saw me looking terrified and confused. She came and took me by the arm.

I recognized the older woman because she ran a bed and breakfast establishment in the outer regions of town. I have even heard my mother speak of this woman. She bent down and looked my face over.

The older woman grabbed my cheeks and squished my face in the way that aunts do at Thanksgiving dinner. I was just so happy to see someone I recognized. I had been panicking before, and she stopped it with her cold arms.

"Ian! There you are!" Called my mother. She looked terrified. She came over to me and grabbed my arm. The old lady grasped the other as my mother tried to drag me away from her. Mom looked back at the woman with rage.

"Let him go, Gloria. Stop being so creepy and let my child go!" My mother said.

"Call the police, I don't care," said the old woman, tightening her grip. My arm began to ache beneath her palm. Some of the staff surrounded us and commanded Gloria to release me. She finally did.

You know just as well as I, that as I got older, I realized no one was after me with machines. No one was going to hunt me down. Except maybe Gloria, the only one in that whole chaotic mess whom I trusted. The woman would eventually find herself in a lot of trouble trying to keep unwilling people for companionship when they'd checked in at her bed and breakfast.

15

TRADING GOODS

There was something wrong with Wavy the Clown. He looked sick. It seemed as though he were sweating through his makeup. My mother and I had noticed this early in the day and had kept an eye on him. My niece's birthday party was going to be memorable.

We watched him juggle. The children would laugh as he dropped pins, thinking that it was part of his act. I believed that he was feeling so unwell that his motor skills were affected.

I was an aspiring magician. I pulled Wavy to the side and told him that I would be happy to finish the party's performance if he was feeling sick. He told me that his company had scheduled a magician to perform after him; he just had to make it until five p.m.

He eventually stumbled away from the front of the young crowd gathered in my cousin's living room. I felt so bad for the guy. The magician took his place in front of the screaming children, not looking much better. Was everyone from the entertainment company sick?

I had been trying to learn magic for years. I had already decided that my stage name was going to be Tanner, the Amazing. Unfortunately, I just could not move my hands quickly enough to be good at the tricks I tried to learn.

I always enjoyed watching another magician at work. This particular performer's name was Josh Spark. The guy was brilliant. He made a rabbit appear from the baseball hat of a guest. I had no idea how he accomplished the trick.

Then, he snapped, and a flower appeared from thin air. Even though he looked a little sickly, he was one of the best live acts that I had ever seen. My niece and the other children were going crazy for his performance.

I could have sworn that I even saw him refill his water glass from nowhere when no one else was looking. I clapped, believing that it was a trick, and he seemed confused. It was then that I realized I had probably just misunderstood.

The magician went on to do so many more incredible tricks; He made a party guest disappear and then reappear. The magician then pulled a coin from the cup of another. There were birds at some point; I was just adored every moment of the performance. I wanted to perfect the same tricks! I would have given almost anything for magic.

When his act ended, he stumbled off the stage. He looked worn out. I was worried that my questions might bother Josh, but I had to let him know how much he had inspired me to keep working.

I found him alone in the kitchen. He was leaning over the counter space as he drank a new glass of water. He looked as though he must be exhausted.

"Hey Josh, I just wanted to tell you that you're the best magician that I believe I have ever seen! I had no idea how you did any of those tricks. You have such a bright future," I said. Josh laughed, but he seemed annoyed.

"Thanks. I did the tricks with magic," he said.

"I am something of an aspiring magician, myself. I honestly could not tell," I replied.

"Wait. You are a magician?" He asked. Suddenly, his whole stance changed. He seemed much more positive. "Why didn't you say so sooner? You know, I can teach you how to perform like me. I could even get you hired by the same company. How would you feel about that?"

"That sounds too good to be true," I said. "I have been working at this for so many years!"

"Is it your passion?" Josh asked.

"I believe so," I said. "I haven't really been interested in other hobbies."

"I can make you the best magician, right now. You would have to sign up with my company first, though. I have two years left on my contract, and I could just give it to you," the magician said.

"Wait, you are giving me *your* actual job? You don't want it?"

"I am just so tired. I need to sign someone else up, and you seem perfect. There is just...one more thing." Josh said. The tone of his voice became frightening.

"Maybe I will do some research and get back to you," I said. I no longer trusted the man in front of me.

"Let me change your mind. My secret on stage is magic. I can do real magic," Josh said. He then proceeded to create an orb of fire the size of a baseball. The magician suspended it in the air in front of him. I gasped. I could not believe my eyes. It had to be a trick. "I can give you my magic."

"What is the catch?" I asked. I was not ready for the answer.

Josh explained that he had to pay his soul for the magic. He now needed to give the spell to someone else before he was sent his bill. Josh's boss was some sort of paranormal creature, according to Josh. He told me that when I accept, his own contract would be extended.

I immediately answered no, I would not pay my soul for anything. Especially not to become a sick traveling magician. He began to advance toward me, telling me that I would regret not taking this chance. I backed up more and more until I was against a wall.

Then his boss walked in as though he had just materialized at the party. The man was almost seven feet tall. He had long black hair and eyes that looked almost black too. Something about his facial features was not quite human. His cheekbones were too sharp, as was his chin. His features looked insidious because of the shadows they cast. I had never been more afraid in my life. I felt like I could not move. Josh told me that there was no way he could let me go after telling me who he was.

The boss just stood in the corner, smiling in a bad way. He held a folder and a pen in one hand, which I assumed was the contract. He was waiting for me to give in, and I didn't feel like I had much of a choice.

The boss held out his arm, offering the folder and pen to me. Just as I was reaching out my hand to take the contract, my mother walked in. She saw the look on my face. She could always tell when something was off.

"Tanner, I think it is time to go. We need to get home," she said. Josh sighed heavily and moved out of my way. The magician realized that he had been beaten. My mother could smell danger like a bloodhound. The boss rolled his eyes. I left with my mother that day, having sold my soul to no one. When we were outside, I threw my arms around her. That was the day that my niece's birthday party almost killed me!

16

THE MELODY

I can still remember being a little brat. I was an awful child. My twin sister and I would fight always, and I would throw ridiculous insults at her. She did the same, as we were pretty standard siblings. I would tell her that she had cooties and she could call me a cry baby.

As I grew older, I came to value our dynamic so much more. Claire and I became the best of friends. We would tell one another everything and still find time for silly insults. We were so close that she moved to a new city so that I wouldn't be alone. She was older, and I guess she felt the need to watch over me. Protect me. I would have called her paranoid only a few months ago, but then Claire saved my life.

One day, my phone rang while I was out walking my dog. I fumbled through my pockets to find the device as my friend took the leash from me. My father was calling.

"Hey, Dennis! For you and Claire's birthday this year, we want to do something exceptional," he said.

"Please don't spend a lot of money on us," I replied.

"Too late! Your mom and I got you guys tickets to a cruise. I know you have never been on a boat before. The trip will be an adventure," he said.

I had never been out of my state before! I fussed at him for spending so much on the present, but I'd be lying if I said I wasn't excited. I called Claire, and she screamed through the other end of the phone line that she had just gotten the news from mom.

We both prepared for weeks before our departure date. The anticipation was killing me. I wanted so badly to see something other than the city. I wanted to relax. It was going to be especially fun with Claire, as she usually pushes me to pursue real adventures. Without her, I would probably have just laid around the entire time.

Our first day on the cruise was terrific. I found out that I get seasick, but there was an easy remedy for that. We listened to music and ate so much good food. I made friends with some other people in the waterpark on top of the boat. I had never realized how massive cruise ships were.

We watched the sunset with our new friends. The painted neon sunset spread out before us, hues of pink and orange swirled together. There was a gentle wind from the forward motion of the boat. It blew against us, carrying the smell of amazing savory food. The sound of the water hitting the ship was almost enough to lull me to sleep.

There was this feeling that went alongside childhood. There were so many new experiences that it was as if the world around you were full of magic. I had not felt that sense of wonder in so long, until the vacation. The days slipped away so quickly.

One night, we were sailing over exotic seas. The scenery was beautiful. There were large limestone rock formations that rose from the sea, like towers. They were so majestic. Small islands popped up around us. The turquoise water expanded out behind the boat, but we were looming closer to land.

By the following morning, we would be able to see our next stop. I had a busy day full dancing and getting to know other people on board. My sister had spent her time in the pool. I arrived back to the cabin first, slinging myself down upon my bed before the twilight had even touched the evening sky.

I awoke in the middle of the night to the motion of the ship. I had a strange feeling in the pit of my stomach. It felt as though I were at the very top of a rollercoaster, and I had just looked down. I thought that I either had a strange dream or my motion sickness was coming back. Either way, I was free to ignore the uneasy feelings.

Then I heard the song. My ears automatically twitched when the sound first rushed over me. It was the most hauntingly beautiful melody I had ever heard. There was nothing to which I could compare this experience.

A smooth feminine voice called out from outside my cabin. The noise was spellbinding. I felt myself rising to my feet. I had to find the location where the beautiful song was reaching out. My body was moving slowly. I did not feel as though I was in control of myself.

My sister called out to me, but I could not answer her. I suppose that all of my movement had woken her from her sleep. At that moment, all I wanted was to find the sound. Every cell in my body wanted to see the music. I opened the door to the cabin slowly.

Claire repeated my name, but I did not heed. I walked down the hallway where our rooms were located, and then up some stairs. I continued to wander about until I found the deck of the boat. The melody was coming from those stony structures in the sea. I felt compelled to jump off the side of the massive ship, but I held myself back.

I saw figures swaying on top of the rock formations. They were glowing blue. Each was wearing a long gown that moved gracefully in the breeze. There were at least three of these creatures. They all began to sing at one time.

Suddenly, my will was not strong enough. I began

to venture toward the edge of the deck. I was going to jump in. I was both excited and intensely frightened.

I leaned over the railing, listening to the sweet song for just a moment longer. It was calling out to me; it wanted me to join. They needed me. It was time.

My sister yanked me backward, and I fell down hard onto the concrete. I was so confused. I could still hear the noise, but it was fading because I wasn't concentrated on it any longer. Claire slapped me, and finally, the sound disappeared.

To this day, she believes that she saved me from sleepwalking. She had no idea the mortal danger that I was actually in that night. The night I tried to reach out to the siren's song.

❧ 17 ❧

A DOLL'S EYES

The Embers family had a lot of strange traditions that Chelsea wondered about. There were so many days designated for weird celebrations. For instance, they always got together to feast on the first day of spring. They called this day "Banquet of Rebirth."

Neither her mother, Ida, nor her grandmother, Gemma, could tell her why they practiced these traditions. The celebrations were passed down through the generations, and somehow, everyone was fine with carrying them on. One can never have too many parties, she supposed.

There was a legend that the family had come from witches. The feasts had been a way of life that just persisted long past the act beliefs. Ida thought that such superstition was silly. She did not even believe in ghosts.

Chelsea was a beautiful girl with curling brown hair and eyes the color of coffee. They even turned the same auburn color when the sunlight reflected off of them. The young lady was her mother's pride and joy, as she was as beautiful inside as out.

One day, Ida received a call from a local museum. They said that they had a doll that was donated by her great grandmother. They were clearing out old attractions to make room and wondered if she might want the heirloom back.

Ida excitedly said yes. She and Chelsea immediately set out to pick up the doll. When they arrived, they were handed a strange glass jar, with the figure inside. The museum told them that it was standard procedure to keep items in thick glass containers. Ida thought nothing of it.

The doll was weathered but still lovely. It had the same dark hair and dark eyes that Chelsea had. It looked a lot like her daughter. Ida thought that it was the coolest item she had ever received, and she was glad to take the artifact home.

Gemma joined the pair at their small brick house upon hearing the news. She was also excited to see the newest addition to the family. The moment she laid eyes on the doll, she shrieked. Ida and Chelsea stared at her with concern upon their faces.

The confused grandmother apologized for yelling. She had no idea why she had such a reaction to seeing a doll. She felt silly but could not help waiting to keep her distance from the thing.

In the following weeks, both Ida and Chelsea would learn that Gemma had a strong intuition. Chelsea slept in her room with the door closed and the fan running on high. She was careful to shut her closet too because it scared her to see it open.

She began to awaken in the middle of the night with her door swung open. The fan would be turned off. The closet door was opened just a crack. Chelsea's heart would sink as she forced herself to get out of bed and check the room.

Ida left the doll in the living room of their home at first. Every morning, she would walk by the figure to see it lying in a different direction. Ida felt as though she were going crazy. She would always fix the doll and then continue going about her day.

Chelsea then began acting weird. She would forget her name, calling herself Blanche, or just wandering around. She was scaring her mother. Finally, she confessed to her mother that the door to her room was opened during the night. Ida eyed the doll.

The pair called Gemma over to their house to explain. The grandmother finally felt validated for her initial reaction to the thing. Ida mentioned that perhaps they could throw the figure away. Gemma said she didn't like that idea.

The grandmother explained her theory. She believed that they had a great great great relative named Blanche. She was not comfortable destroying the doll until they understood what was happening.

They called a spiritual advisor from in town, someone that Gemma's friends recommended. The woman was very extraordinary. She was older, but she spoke with slang from the eighties. She wore her crimped white hair in a side ponytail. Ida was immediately concerned.

"Alright, let me meet her," those were her first words to the family.

"Who? Chelsea?" Asked Ida, pointing to her daughter.

"No, the doll," said the spiritual advisor.

She spent hours sitting on their faux leather couch, just staring at the doll. She was making direct eye contact with the thing; she whispered to her mother that the woman needed to leave. It was around that time that she broke from her gaze.

"There is a ghost trapped inside of this doll. It is a relative named Blanche. She likely cast the spell upon herself to claim a young member of the family. I suppose you guys were just lucky enough to pick the wrong generation. She wants out, and she wants your daughter," said the woman. "She is going to go mental until she gets what she wants."

"Is there nothing else that we can do?" Asked

Gemma. Chelsea could not believe what she was hearing. Was someone trying to steal her body? Not only that, but they had magic on their side.

Chelsea had never felt so helpless in her entire life. She began to shake and cry. Was her body going to be taken away from her, piece by piece? A knot emerged in the pit of her stomach. She had no idea what to do. She was doomed, no matter what.

Ida put her arms around her daughter. She was not going to let the ghost get away with the attack. She would not let anyone hurt Chelsea.

"I will burn it," said Gemma.

"No, don't. The doll has already traded some of its soul. You would be getting rid of a part of your daughter," said the woman. Chelsea wept. "Don't worry. There are a few options. I have a solution that might hold for a while. We will discuss in the other room,"

The following day, Chelsea came home with blue hair. Bright blue. Huge thick glasses hung over her nose. The spiritual advisor figured that if the doll waited this long for the best looking relative, that she could be vain. She believed that Blanche would back off if Chelsea were unattractive to her. She used to look almost exactly like the young girl.

When she decided that she did not want Chelsea to be her host, they could burn the doll. Surprisingly, the plan worked perfectly. Gemma, Ida, and Chelsea all stood by the fire, warming their hands. At that moment, they all felt connected to their family's witchy past.

❧ 18 ❧

DEAD HEAT

I have heard people say that the Vestford Estate had a ghost problem. The family that lived there was a little odd, but most super-rich people were. I know they couldn't keep help, and there were a lot of rumors as to why. My father said they paid well, so I knew that wasn't causing their turn-over issue.

He said that a maid that used to work for the family said that weird things happen on the estate at night. Lots of loud noises kept everyone awake. She was frightened by a ghostly figure shooting across the lawn in the early hours of dawn. The woman thought that she might be going mad; she turned in her resignation letter shortly after.

My father was going to be working for the family full time. He was to be a personal assistant to the entire household. They told him that they mainly just needed another person around to fill-in where needed. They gave us a cushy apartment in the eastern wing of their estate. We moved in right as summer started.

"Tom," said my father, "you will never believe where we are going to live!" The apartment that we had called home for almost two years was in rough shape. The neighbors spent all night screaming at one another. There was a new leak every week, it seemed. The air conditioner was engaged in a constant crisis of conscience; it didn't know if it would rather watch us suffer through the heat entirely or if it should offer us false hope first. So, I was excited to hear any answer other than "right here, again. Forever."

Apparently, according to my father, the family gained their wealth through oil generations ago. The Vestfords were farmers that struck oil while digging a well for their tiny (then) new home. They shot up through society.

With every new generation, their money became a little older. The Vestford Family became a little more sophisticated. The Vestfords involved themselves a little more, into high society, and all of its pastimes.

The family gained national attention in the 1920s for having a very successful racehorse named Hemlock. The animal became a household name and added even more wealth and fame to the Vestford name. There was a museum dedicated to Hemlock, located on the property.

I didn't know much about horses, but I joined my father at their estate to learn. I had just turned sixteen, so the family was going to allow me to work for them. I was going to help the serving staff when it came time for meals.

I had so far only gotten to meet two members of the family. The father's name was Richard. He was intellectual and incredibly kind. I had expected the man to be closed off and cruel, but he was the opposite. His wife, Holly, was not my favorite person.

They had two children around my age. I had yet to see either of them around, but I imagined that they would make an appearance before summer was through. The other staffers were friendly enough. I had yet to make any real friends, but I was also just starting.

My first few weeks living at the estate were chaotic. Settling into a new home can be a lot, on its own. I also had a new job where I needed to learn the ropes. I was grateful for my new surroundings and looked forward to my first summer not spent in a tiny old city apartment.

Richard took the time to get to know me. He reminded me a lot of my father. The two of us played pool in the evenings sometimes. We spoke of books and history. I asked a lot of questions about his family and their timeline. I was especially interested in Hemlock.

Richard told me that his grandfather's heart broke when the horse ran away. Richard explained that his grandfather treated Hemlock like another member of their family. The man had even had a portrait commissioned of the two of them together. Richard was making the image from the painting made into a statue for the front of the estate.

As I walked along the gilded hallways, across the marble floors, I could not help but imagine Richard's grandfather. The interior of their mansion was so fancy. I pictured a cultured older man with a cigar and a thick beard. That was until Richard showed me the portrait.

The man looked a little devious. I hate to think ill of the dead, but there was none of the kindness in the grandfather's face that I had seen in Richard's. The grandfather looked cold and distant.

Sometimes, during the night, I would be awoken by a bang. I knew enough of the city to recognize that it was a gunshot. I would hear lots of other strange sounds that sent my thoughts racing.

I felt terror crawling all over my body as I sat up in bed one night. Frightening sounds were coming from outside. I stood up and put on my slippers to inspect, even though my heart was already beating far too fast. My face was hot, and my breathing was only growing heavier.

I heard what I believed to be the sound of a whip. I looked outside the window to see only darkness. Sleep evaded me that night, but when it finally came, I had a strange dream.

The man from the portrait was rushing about the hallways, and I was following him. Occasionally, he would bark orders at me in a language that I could not understand. He became so frustrated with me that he stopped in his tracks. We were standing in the library when he halted.

The man produced a whip, hitting me several times. I screamed. I cried. I begged for mercy. The leather stung my skin like a burn. He just would not stop. Richard's grandfather then told me to follow him, and he kicked a panel of wood on the end of a random bookcase. The piece popped out, revealing a makeshift safe, a hiding place.

I awoke from my dream, sweating and frightened, only to hear another sound coming from outside. I looked out once more. On the lawn stood a glowing horse. I knew that it was Hemlock. He reared up on his hind legs.

Something told me not to be afraid. I grabbed my slippers and raced through the massive hallways, then down the grand staircase. I was worried that Hemlock was going to be gone by the time I arrived outside. The horse was still there.

The horse began to jog off toward a wooded area. I followed him, having to run as fast as I could to keep up. The dew dampened the grass. I held my arms out to keep my balance. The night air was cool against my skin, even though it was the middle of summer.

I followed the beautiful glowing horse into the forest. Hemlock slowed so that I could catch up. He finally stopped in front of a large boulder. The animals looked at me, looked through me. His eyes were so full of hurt that I wanted to sob.

Hemlock struggled to lay himself down upon the ground before disappearing. I understood his message. The moment was so severe and silent. I awoke in my bed, wondering if the entire ordeal had been a dream. I knew that the library scene was in my head, but following the ghost-horse felt real.

I got myself dressed that day to take a walk. I didn't tell anyone where I was going. I made my way out to the woods. The sun was shining; birds chirped happy tunes from every direction. The mood was much different than it was in my dream, but that same boulder laid right in front of me.

I found Richard in his study. I knocked lightly on the doorframe, getting his attention. I asked him to come with me to the library.

I warned Mr. Vestford that he might not like what he sees. He was confused by my statements but allowed me to continue. I found the same bookcase that his grandfather had tapped in my dream. The panel popped out, just as it had before.

Richard was so excited to find journals from his grandfather. I warned him again. I then retreated to my room so that he could read.

His grandfather was not a good man. Richard explained that the journals detailed his disdain for Hemlock. He was cruel to the creature, enforcing his will with whips and yelling. His wife had cared for the horse, so he promised her that he would keep the animal even after he stopped being useful on the track.

Richard's grandfather did not keep that promise. Hemlock was buried beneath the oblong boulder. I told Richard of my dreams, and the man broke down. He could not believe that such an honored member of their family was handled so poorly. His love for animals was admirable.

Mr. Vestford immediately called the statue makers. He declared that he would like the monument forged to Hemlock, alone. Richard also created a headstone for the horse, which he visited often. Something must have happened in the Vestford bloodline. Richard was a good man, perhaps one of the best I had ever met.

✻ 19 ✻

ONE WHOLE BAT

Lilah was an earth witch. Everything about her life was green, except for her skin. Most of the spells that she used called for plants and herbs. She lived in a feudal era kingdom. Magic of all kinds was declared evil, long ago.

By living deep within an enchanted forest and only using plants for her spells, Lilah managed to keep herself off the king's radar. He was looking for evil witches doing crazy magic. She was not taking anything from the king's land, and she was not using offensive chants. Lilah never even left her little section of the woods.

Lilah lived off of the earth, and her passion was nature. Her diet was completely dependent on her garden; she even created her own clothing from plants. Lilah had one personal rule that she could do no harm to other living creatures.

Lilah lived a beautiful life. She didn't have any mortal friends, but others were overrated. She was never truly alone, after all. The witch's best friend was a sweet raccoon that sometimes helped her look for her ingredients in the forest. She had never even cast a spell on the creature.

She did not want her life to change. Lilah wanted to go on living on her own and minding her business for as long as fate would allow. Unfortunately, fate did not approve.

Lilah got horrible news by way of messenger dove form her father. Lilah's mother had been lost in the Long Mountains. The pair had not spoken in years, but she could not just let her mother remain exposed to the elements. She was going to have to act. Her father was a mortal, so there was little that he could do on his own, she suspected.

The young witch quickly found a spell attached to the back of the letter. The only outlying ingredient it called for was one whole bat. Her heart dropped. There were no bats in her forest; the fairies ran them away. She would have to venture into the king's land.

There was a sense of dread that filled Lilah's chest as she mounted her horse. She would have to hope that she was not spotted taking a bat from the king's cave. Lilah was going to have to take the risk; there was no other choice.

Lilah rode her horse through the magical forest and then entered the king's land. An ivy gate appeared at the border of the two woodlands, meant to keep mortals out of the enchanted side. Panels of vines pulled apart from each other, like laced fingers coming undone, to allow the young witch.

Lilah continued upon the doomed path. She quickly found a cave and set to work stealing a bat. The job turned out to be much more complicated than she had initially anticipated.

Lilah could feel something watching her, as she tried to leave the king's forest. Even the trees seemed more threatening there. They swayed in toward Lilah with their leafy branches reaching out like hands. They looked as though they were going to grab her.

Lilah felt her heart begin to race. She felt as though she could not move, but she was going to have to carry on. Lilah held on tight as her horse broke out into a dead sprint. She knew that running was only going to encourage her paranoia.

Then she heard rustling all around her. The trees obscured her view, but something was coming for her. It was keeping up with her. Lilah could do nothing except to try to run her horse faster.

Finally, she reached the ivy boundary gate. It opened for her and then slammed closed directly behind her. The weak bat in her bag must have been terrified.

"I know you don't believe me, but I am not going to hurt you," she said to her bag. "I will get you back home safe when all this is over."

Lilah quickly performed the spell, upon returning home. It required the bat to circle the room three times. Getting the bat to fly in a coordinated manner was also a difficult task. Before the magical map illustrating her mother's location, had even dried from the spell, she handed it off to the carrier dove. The bird would deliver the document to her father. The witch knew that she must prepare for her arrest.

The young witch readied herself and bundled her bat friend up in a cloth so he wouldn't fly away before she had him back to his cave. She hugged her raccoon companion and then looked at her beautiful mossy hut, one last time. Lilah had not been given a choice in any of this. She had morals that she had to adhere to, no matter the cost.

She crossed back over into the king's land, on the back of her horse. Lilah returned to the bat's cave; unwrapping was her swaddle to set the animal-free. Early into Lilah's journey back home, she was stopped by a confused knight.

The knight was wearing dark chainmail with a massive sword by his side; he was a terrifying sight for the small witch. She questioned her silly morals; she should not have returned to this land. Then she noticed the knight's hand. He held the map that she had created for her father so he could find her mother.

"No! I know you are going to arrest me. That's

fine. Please let that map go to my father. He needs it-" Lilah started to explain.

"No, she doesn't," said the knight, cutting her off.

"Yes, you don't understand. She is lost in the mountains and-"

"No. We set you up," The knight said. There was no emotion in the knight's voice. Lilah was too stunned to speak; she had not interacted with other humans often. She had forgotten their nature.

"Why?" She finally asked after a long silence.

"The king wants to expand his land," said the knight.

"Why not just ask me to move? Are you going to take my freedom? I would have left my home to keep my freedom." Lilah said. The young witch was hurt and confused.

"I am just following orders," said the knight. The knight took the sad witch into custody, but he let her ride her horse. The pair rode in silence toward the mortal hunting grounds.

"You know the enchanted forest isn't going to let the king enter, right?" Said, Lilah.

"I figured as much when it would not let me enter to arrest you," said the knight. "But that is none of my concern."

"Are you going to hurt me?" Said the frightened witch. Lilah was shaking uncontrollably. The thought of someone hurting her to steal her land terrified her. What would someone capable of an action such as that, do to her. She was going to be locked in the tower.

Lilah knew the future before her. Through the sparse trees in the remaining patch of forest, she could see the castle. It was a dark and scary place. The building was tall, imposing, and made of sharp angles meant to intimidate.

"Look, I didn't want anything to do with this. I only follow orders. We all have to do things we don't want. I am not going to hurt you. I can't promise the prison won't, but I am not. If you had not left the enchanted side of the forest, this would not be an issue. You would be safe, and no one would be able to arrest you. I tried to enter behind you; I absolutely could not get through. You could have been safe," said the knight. "Why did you leave?"

"I am afraid a man like you would not understand," Lilah said. She felt as though she might throw up. She had never been so terrified.

"That is rich coming from a tree witch who was arrested for sacrificing a bat for some kind of evil magic," said the knight. The witch laughed bitterly. The kingdom looked down on her. No matter how kind she was. No matter how hard she tried.

"Are you all so uninformed? One whole bat? You stole that spell from someone to give to me, right?" Lilah asked.

"Yes, I had to. The king gave the order to-"

"Well, for next time, One Whole Bat means that

the bat lives. It stays whole; I would not have used your dumb spell, otherwise. It's a WHOLE BAT. We use the energy created as it flies around the room in a circle.

"Furthermore, I left the enchanted forest to return the bat. The bat is fine. I even fed him," Lilah said.

"Wait? The bat isn't dead?" Asked the knight, stopping the horses.

"No, the bat is fine," Lilah said.

"The arrest warrant was issued for the slaying of an animal from the king's property. I will let you go now if you run home and never speak of this to anyone. From now on, if you are sent a message through carrier dove, hold it to the sun. If royal stationery had been used, a crown would appear in the back. Never tell a soul about this, or you will have killed me," said the knight.

"Thank you," Lilah said. Tears ran down her face. She could not stop crying. The knight let go of the reins from her horse. The green witch rode back into the forest from which she came.

❧ 20 ❧

LET'S SPLIT UP

Leonie was referred to as "Leo" by her friends. The nickname a convenient shortening of her actual name, and it was also a nod to her adventurous nature. She was the lioness in charge of her small group of friends, and she was not afraid of anything.

Greg was determined to take Leo's place in the hearts of their peers. He was always a little jealous that he could not take his position as the resident cool guy. Greg liked sports and told offensive jokes, but he was also genuinely caring.

Kev was a smart guy. He was a little shy and had a hard time asserting himself. Whenever anyone had a homework question, they turned to Kev. He was a mathlete.

Portia, the final friend in their small clique, was intelligent. She was also a little moody, but somehow, she fit right in with her closest companions. They would have never been friends if they had not worked together with each other, the summer before. Now, they were all unified.

They had all taken to the open road in Greg's car. It had to the most room to stretch out. They were going on a small road trip to include a handful of states that none of the group had ever seen.

Most of their stops were pretty standard. They would always find something to poke fun at, earning them some annoyance from locals. They visited the World's Largest Toothpick, and none of them could hold their laughter.

"It's a tree," said Greg. He was already fighting a smile. The roadside attraction's attendant looked confused for a moment.

"No, sir, it is meant to be a toothpick," the attendant said.

"It is a tree. You guts have just cut off the branches and the bark. Now you charge people to see it, and we fell for it," Portia said.

"If you don't like the toothpick, feel free to leave. Most people just take a picture with it," said the lady.

"Guys! Stop laughing. She is right. Who wants their picture taken with the tree?" Asked Leo. Kev apologized on behalf of the group as they left.

When it was Greg's turn to drive, the friends decided to take the particularly scenic road. Rolling hills rose and fell to the side of the car. Lush green trees seemed to wave as the wind danced through them. Everyone in the car was quiet because they had already had such a long day.

The road continued for an eternity. The friends had chosen the wrong path. The car was running low on gas, and there was nowhere to stop. There was no anything. No shops, no restaurants. The friends were beginning to push the vehicle to its limits.

A creepy lone building stood on the horizon on the top of a hill. The exterior was worn down. It looked like a two-story farmhouse, but there was a sign on a stand, in the front yard, that said something. As they got closer, they could see that it said "Hotel/ Bed and Breakfast." They had no choice.

An older lady met them at the front door; she watched them pull up the huge driveway. She gave the appearance of a normal grandmother, but something was strange. The friends could feel it. She agreed to see that they got gas the following morning, which was beyond kind.

The friends were assigned to one of two rooms on the second story of the house. When they returned to the car to retrieve their belongings, the "Hotel" sign was gone. Kev told his friends that something was wrong. Everyone agreed, even Leo.

The lady made the friends diner. They were all starving, but Kev was reluctant to eat her food. It seemed like four different kinds of mush. He pretended to take a few bites, miming the motions.

That night, as the group settled into their beds, there was a general feeling of unease. Leo was the first to fall asleep. A loud banging sound awoke her. The room was completely dark, and the noise was coming from the hallway.

Kev and Greg ran from their own room to Leo and Portia's. They were terrified. They felt as though they were being watched as they dashed. The noise rang out through the darkness.

"Should one of us go and see what is making the sound?" Asked Portia.

"I will go," replied.

"No. Listen. We aren't stupid. No one is splitting up; we can't. We are not going to make any of the awful decisions that people do in the movies. We stick together," Kev said. Leo was impressed that he spoke up.

The friends decided to move one of the beds against the door so that they had more time to think. The bangs were growing louder and louder. They all listened in horror as the source of the sound crept closer.

The wood on their door began to bow as the something outside battered against it. A horrible screeching came from the other side. Leo searched for her phone, but it was nowhere. Portia had the same problem. They had been sleeping so hard.

"Guys, I think we were drugged at dinner. I fell

asleep, and now I can't find my phone," said Leo softly. The horrible noise consumed everything.

"That makes sense! The lady tried to come into our room, but I had only pretended to eat, so I was awake. I did eventually fall asleep, though. I don't have my phone either," said Kev. "She probably wouldn't be banging if she hadn't stolen them."

"Yeah, she stole one of mine too," whispered Greg.

"One!? Please tell me you have one!" said Portia. Greg pulled a cell phone from his sock.

"I don't want to know why you have that, but you are a hero Greg!" whispered Leo. She could not see him blush in the dark.

"It is for the basketball teammates. They need to always be able to reach me," Greg said before calling the police.

"YOU WON'T STAY IN THERE FOREVER!" Screamed the woman.

"You're right. We need ten more minutes, and we will come out willingly! We will surrender. Is that okay?" Asked Leo

"NOW!"

The friends managed to keep the woman busy with talking for just long enough. Blue lights reflected off the walls in their room, from the outside. The woman could not see the lights because she was so glued to their door.

She was such an unassuming maniac. Upon her arrest, the police discovered that she was keeping other people in her basement. They were locked up and unable to leave. She had a murderous fear of being alone.

The friends had resisted the urge to separate and investigate. They called for help. They were the first of her guests to not fall into her trap. Kev somehow just knew she was evil, all along. The real hero, though, was Greg's second phone.

CPSIA information can be obtained
at www.ICGtesting.com
Printed in the USA
LVHW040040290422
717483LV00008B/1329